I REMAIN,
YOUR UNCLE
AMBROGIO

I REMAIN, YOUR UNCLE AMBROGIO

Mangiapelo, Ambrogio, 1894-

(GENE HORWITZ)

Henry Regnery Company · Chicago

Library of Congress Cataloging in Publication Data

Mangiapelo, Ambrogio, 1894-
    "I remain, your Uncle Ambrogio."

    Letters.
    1. Mangiapelo, Ambrogio, 1894-   2. Horwitz,
Gene.   I. Horwitz, Gene.   II. Title.
CT275.M4553A44   1975   973.9'092'4 [B]
ISBN 0-8092-8195-3   75-14216

Copyright © 1975 by Gene Horwitz
All rights reserved
Published by Henry Regnery Company
180 North Michigan Avenue, Chicago, Illinois 60601
Manufactured in the United States of America
Library of Congress Catalog Card Number: 75-14216
International Standard Book Number: 0-8092-8195-3

Published simultaneously in Canada by
Fitzhenry & Whiteside Limited
150 Lesmill Road
Don Mills, Ontario M3B 2T5
Canada

For Uncle Ambrogio
and
For Noni

Introduction

Uncle Ambrogio came to America from Italy (Province of Frosinone) in 1912 at the age of 18. His formal education ended at the third-grade level in Italy, and when he reached adulthood he began a self-improvement crusade that is still going on at age 81. With dogged determination and painstaking effort he has taught himself to read and write both English and Italian. Hours were spent with his dictionary, first-grade readers, and spelling books. He went on to the study of the daily paper and crossword puzzles. My earliest recollections are of him poring over lists of words, writing them over and over. He studied the homework we brought home from school in the 1930s and 1940s and was still studying homework my son brought home from school 20 years later.

He taught himself to read music and play the accordion. He became proficient at electrical work, plumbing, gardening, painting, carpentry, mechanics, cement and construction work, and at 75 he took up drawing and painting. He single-handedly built a small home during one summer season when he was in his early 50s.

I have never heard him raise his voice in anger or say an unkind word to or about anyone. He has always been loving and thoughtful, and even his saddest moments are laced with humor. I have never received a letter from him that didn't make me smile—sometimes happily, sometimes sadly, but still a smile.

In this book my mother is referred to as "You Mother," "Noni," "Mom," "Virginia," and "Mama." His devotion to her during her last years as an invalid can never be repaid. Their understanding of each other is difficult to describe, but it does show through in his letters. Her humor matched his, and both used it to help each other. They would spend an entire evening together without conversation except for an occasional comment made to the ceiling. For example, Mom, looking up at the ceiling, would say: "Some people who are healthy and can eat anything they want have no understanding heart." Uncle Ambrogio, looking at the same ceiling: "Some people who have enlarge heart and get sick from eating have no understanding."

My mother did not have the benefit of any education at all but managed to raise a large family, learned to speak English by listening, and ran a neighborhood grocery store while learning the language and the rate of exchange. In spite of living with constant pain and discomfort during her last years, she maintained an indomitable spirit that could never be broken, and she was a strong, driving force behind all of us. She also suffered the pain of divorce before her children were grown, an unheard of thing in her home country. She made the difficult adjustment to liberal thinking through personal associations in this country and later on through watching television.

Her five children, referred to in this book, are Yolanda (Yola), Albert (Al, Bertie), Rose, myself (Gina), and her youngest, Virginia (Gee Gee).

I have put down these letters and memories so that my children will accurately remember Uncle Ambrogio and their "Noni." I don't want them to be dependent on memories alone, which are inclined to fade and become distorted with the years.

I have not made any attempt to correct Uncle Ambrogio's misspellings, misquotations, or errors in punctuation for fear of losing the flavor and beautiful simplicity of his writing. Many of the bigger words are spelled correctly, while some of the smaller ones are not. On the other hand, certain words are spelled correctly sometimes but at other times they are not. This apparently depends on his mood at the time and whether or not he wants to look up the words he is not sure of. He also has his warm-up exercises to go through before starting a letter. He doodles on a pad to get the feel of the pen, circles the air over the paper like a pitcher warming up, and then he's ready to write with a very precise, jagged scrawl.

Of course, there are things about him these letters do not tell. How he throws his head back when he laughs and bows it sadly when he is disappointed or sad. His silent courage through his own pain and suffering. His loyalty, integrity, and simple goodness. A beautiful man, my Uncle Ambrogio, also known as Uncle Boo, Bruno, Zio, 300, 210, and 510.

This treasure to me and mine he would only call "Le mei povere e semplici parole" . . . "My poor and simple words."

Part I

Dear Gina,

How sad that you are move away, but one good thing is I will now have opportunity to say only the things what count and not waste lot of words what mean nothing It hurt you Mother now that she never learn to write but I do for both of us.

You are barely gone and I think of many things I wish I have said when you are sit with me. Already I have remember many stories and I think, have I tell that to Gina? I may have lil troubel to tell it. However is a good chance to find what I have learn since I leave the third grade in Italy many years ago. May not sound like much but very few from our little town even reach that and I am one of the lucky one.

Now you are the only one far away from all of us. This will give you time to think of you own stories you want to pass on to you children. Then when they have move away you dont wonder like I do, have I tell this to Gary and Wendy and Lori? You tell now.

I miss you. With lots love I remain,

Your Uncle Ambrogio

Dear Gina,

Here I am—it's me, your Zio, to letting you know how fine we all are at the present time with the esseption of your Great Uncle Severino if you remember him who he was. Is my sad duty to let you know he is passed away at age 77, which is not too bad, and also if you don't remember him you have nothing to fill bad about so I hope you don't remember him very much. The sad thing that happen to him was he was all the time worrying here in America that when the time came he want to die in the old country. So he go back to Roma and was feeling fine when he left here. He is not there more than two three weeks when he get sick and die. Is shame he did not put the trip off few years more.

Well, lets speak about the weather a little bit, which it is not so good here and I am hoping it is better there. Enough about that.

I put one trap out for the squirrel who is getting all the walnuts on the big tree. I had one little accident in the branches with some scretch on my nose and face, and the squirrel I still see run beck and forth across the strit with his arms full of nuts. So he is smarter than I am so far.

I remain,

Your Uncle Ambrogio who send you big kees

Dear Gina,

I gotta repeat conversashun between me and you Mama before I forget it. I don't think you gonna believe it, and I want a witness right away. A loser always looke for a witness, don't they? We are sittin quiet. All of sudden she say "What you want?" and from there we proceed like this.
"I don't want nothing."
"What kind of person not want nothing?"
"Well right now I am person that don't want nothing."
"If you don't want nothing, that mean you are dead person."
"O.K. I am dead person."
"How you think I feel sittin in here all alone with dead person?"
"You want me to leave til I think of something I want?"
"If you got try to think of something you want then you don't really want it."
"O.K. I don't really want it."
"What you don't want?"
"Nothing, thats what I don't want."
"Well, that is what you got — nothing."
"Nothing is what I want in the first place."
"See? You did want something."

Now what I want is for you to write and explain this, that is what I want.

Your loving Uncle Ambrogio,

A dead person

Dear Gina,

Much time have pass since you hear from me because I have not written since then. My reason is that I have been painting the house inside and out — mostly inside because outside the weather is not so good for painting. I have start the picket fence which was white and is now part pink. You Mother she no like the pink I put so while the weather is clearing up I have time to decide wether to paint the pink part white again or go ahead with the pink on the half which is white. She say pink is not for a fence outside. I say she will have only house in town with pink fence outside and she say she will break my head, so I think I will probly decide to paint the pink part white again in which case I will have a fence with one half which is more white than the other, depend on how the sun is shining.

Other than this we are fine and send to you lots kees and love to the kids and Earl.

I remain,

Your Uncle Ambrogio

Dear Gina,

I am sitting here in the kitchen window looking out to admire my white fence which is looking very nice on this end and not so good on the other which I am glad I cannot see from here.

When I am not writing to you I am practising my spalling which I am not getting any better with it but am feeling good to know I am try just as hard as if I was. They have crazy words in this spalling book that I have a time to keep strait in my head. They have in here cheep and cheap. They have also to, too and two. I should say that they have too, too, which will help me to remember which one is which one. I have more trubel with them little words like to than with the big ones like especalle and avengally which I can know right away. However I am making good progress as you can see by the way I spall progress without bit of trubel. That is pretty good because after all I am only 55 years in this country.

I remain your smart Uncle,

Ambrogio

My Dear Knees,

I start out with a little joke there since you make comment on my spalling the words that sound the same. To throw you for loop I also spell "spelling" wrong this time so when I am completely smart I can sneek up on you with it.

We had the family come to eat with us and after dinner I think I would like to entertain them with a little accordian music. After all, I spend many year teach myself to play this thing and read the music and I dont want waste it, you see? I also dont want to look like show off with it so I try to lead up to the subject in a gentel way. I mengen I learn two new songs. Then I mengen that I practise them all week but no play them for anybody yet. Then I say, "I think I go get my accordian", and you Mother say "Why?" and spoil the whole thing. But I got it anyway and play for a while and everyone say it was very good wether they thout so or not.

Everyone here is healthy which I hope you are the same.

Adio,

Uncle Ambrogio

Dear Gina,

I have one funny story to tell you which I think you will get big kick out of it. A salesman from vacume cleaner company come to the door and you Mother answer. She already have same kind vacume and she hate it because it is not easy to pull around and she can not ever take it apart since she have it. He say to her "Good morning I am cleaner man" and she grab him by the shirt and pull him in the house and say "I been waitin for you." Then she make him vacume whole place for her and take the machine apart to clean it. He was so glad to get out of here and I know he will never come back again. The house is nice and clean and so is machine.

You sister Gee Gee come to visit you Mother yesterday. She come to help her with the house and cooking but she walk all the way over and was so tire when she get here that you Mother make lunch for her and then make her take nep on the couch. Then I drive her home.

My car is hold up all right althou is run better in the daytime than at night.

> Resposto pronto.
> Love and kees,
>
> Your Uncle Ambrogio

Dear Gina,

    We were have lots trubel with the boys from the school across the strit. They come sit on the front porch to eat their lunch and they leave such a big mess every day it make you Mother mad and I got to put on lots of time to clean it up every day. So I make a sign that say DO NOT SIT HERE BY ORDER POLIS DEPARTAMENT and pretty soon is come one of the boys to front door and ring the bell. He say to me "You spell polis wrong" and I got to laugh and then he laugh and he leave and they dont sit on the porch no more. So you see the sign work just the same. I forget to ask him how to spell polis.

    You Mother is sit by the kitchen window all day long look out to watch the people go by since she can't walk too much to do nothing else. Every day comes by young boy who wave at her and she wave at him. He is come same time every day and one day he no come and she worry about him. She come in dining room say to me "He's not come by" and she wonder what is wrong. There is tap at the door and is the boy and he say "I no see you in the window and I think something is wrong" and you Mother say "That's what you get for be late — you make us both upset." They laugh lots and he go and they still don't ask each other name but they still wave every day. I think maybe they are both a lil bit pazzo.

    The figs they are ripe on the tree in front and every day you Mother say to me "Go sweep up the rotten ones that fall before somebody slip on them and sue you." She is saying that for 25 years. I hope one of these days it happen so she shut up about it. Until then I remain,

                           Your Uncle Ambrogio

Dear Gina,

You Mother she is sitting in the living room poutin. Today I have take her to the doctor and whatever day this fall on is the day she sit in the living room poutin. After he is examine her he bring her to waiting room where I am waiting, and he is bawl her out like usual for how heavy she is. He say to her "Momma you are obese." She turn to me whisper "Whats a bese?" I say to her "That means you are fat." She say "Then why he no tell me I'm fat?" It so happen he is also fat, and he make the mistake of say to her next "We must do something about your obesty" and she say "OK you do something about yours and I do something about mine." He doesn't think this is so funny. Then she ask him could she have operation to take away the fat and he say "Yes, I could put six stitch across you lips" and ever since then the lips they are press together in this pout. She no eat lunch when we get home, she no eat dinner tonight, she no have no sneck like she likes and I have no peace. Im also very hungry because when she no eat I am afraid to and we are both starve away her obesty. I am now feel to week to continue, so I close now and go faind on my bed.

                    Your loving Uncle Ambrogio who
                    will starve to death very soon

Dear Gina,

    This one she's gonna take me long time to write because I have story for you on you Mother which happen long time ago. You no tell her I tell you or she break my hands.

    She used get so mad when on Sunday you Father he work in the yard because on Sunday nobody should work. So on Sunday he is out in the garden clean around the tomato plants and you Mother is so mad on him she no want talk to him but she want him to know how she feel. So she go out on the porch and look up on the sky and say in very loud voice "Well God, you forgive him because he is stupido and he no care if he go to Hell or not." And you Father he stop working and look up to the sky and say "All right God, I tell you what I'm gonna do. You come down during the week and give me a hands and I no work on Sunday." You Mother is so mad she go in the house and you brother decide he add to the trubel and he is plug in the toaster which go ding ding like the bell in church. So each time the toaster go ding ding he is hit his chest and say "Have mercy on us." You sister is hide and laff like crazy and you Mother she get more mad each minit. Pretty soon you Father come in and he no want talk direct to her so he say in loud voice "I hope there is some grass on the table tonight." This is what he call vegatable. Come five oclock everybody come to the tabel which is set beautiful but on each plate is only handsfull grass. I mean the real grass from the lawn. You Mother she is sit with big steak in front of her and is say "Thank you Lord for take care of you own." We are all sit like bunch dummy lookin at the grass on the dish. You Father no work on Sunday after that and you brother quit play with the toaster. I do nothing but I suffer with the rest, which was worth to have story like this. Such a memory is worth plate full of grass.

> With kees and love I remain,
>
> Uncle Ambrogio

Dear Gina,

I am go crazy with these darn kids from the school across the strit. Seem like every place we live we are near school and get lots trubel. When you were small and go to grade school we are right next to Benjamin Franklin School which you Mother is call Frankaleen Benjaleen all those years but people seem to know what she is talking about just the same.

If you remember the big house we have with attik with two small rooms up there and slant roof. Albert have bedroom up there and he use to climb out the window and slide down roof to the apple tree then climb down and fall to ground and stay out all night. You Mother get suspizus when he start to go to bed every night at 8:30. She say to herself something is feeshy, so she go check on him one night and he is gone. She know he have to come in the same way he went out so she put big white sheet on herself and wait under apple tree. Pretty soon he is come and she wave the arms and go "Ooooh oooh" to him. He go up the tree so fast and up the roof and in the window like he is shot from gun. Next morning he come down and you Mother is make breakfast and she say to him "You no look so good this morning — you pale as sheet — you look like you see ghost or something." He look at her with cow eyes and he know the game is up and that was the end of it. She no have to lift a finger cept to go "oooh oooh" a little bit. Up to then he think he is the smart one. Some time now he think he still is and she wave the arms and go "oooh oooh" to him and he shut up right away like I do now.

With lots love I still remain,

Your Uncle Ambrogio

Dear Gina,

I am sittin with you Mother and she is look on the Sunday paper and show me beautiful picture of sheep and she say "Look on the sheeps." I say to her "You mean sheep—not sheeps." And she say to me "Well, smotty—they are *two*." I stop right there because she is so proud I no wanna smash it for her. I say "Oh, yeah." I don't want her to give me the same trubel she give the Judge when she go for citizenship paper. She study for long time — learn all about constitution and George Washingtone and everybody til she know all the answer. Then she go to the Court and she can not write her name and the Judge say because of that she can't be citizen, and she holler to him, "You no wan me? Go to Hell! I no wan you either! I tell you what you can do with you George Washingtone and you constitshuna and all the rest!" I dont know why she dont land in jail for talk to Judge that way. Then every year for next 50 years she is cuss him out when she have to register for alien.

She no understand card games so good and one day you sister Gee Gee is sittin here play solitare and you Mother say "What you doing?" and Gee Gee say "Playing solitare" and you Mother she say in sad voice "All by youself?!" We dont dare to laugh or she kill us both. Some time is very hard to keep the mouth shut. I gonna shut mine now for while and give you rest from all this nunsense.

Adio, with love and kees,

Your Uncle Ambrogio

Dear Gina,

The time is here for another lettera which I write with specialle care so you can read it. We had surprise visit last week from old friends from Illinois that we did not see for 15 years. They are pop in on us unespette and what shock to see them. They are stay several hour and we talk old times and lots of good laugh over the old days and enjoy ourselves very much. The man is very tall and thin called Waldo and the wife had very bad teeth in front with horn glass on her eyes. Do you know who they are? We are go crazy try to remember them with no luck so far, so if you know you will let us know and turn on the light.

You brother he is fine and you sister Gee Gee is also fine. Everyone else must be fine also because I don't hear that they are not, which is good news.

I say goodby for now, so adio.

I remain,

Your Uncle Ambrogio

Dear Gina,

Non ne posso piu.* I am sitting tired from planting the artifishal flowers all morning in the front. The garlic I plant long time ago have come up there and you Mamma she is asking me what are them plants in the front. When I tell her is the garlic she call me many kind stupido because it does not look so nice in front of the yard. So I go buy some deinty flower to put there and I am all morning tye them on the garlic plants while she is sit in the window watch me like forman. I feel sorry for the people who go to smell them flowers. They are going to get one big surprize. In the meantime as the garlic they get taller the flowers will go higher and bend over and I will have to go out and tye them lower in which case the garlic will avengally be taller than the flowers and then I got to go buy taller flowers. The money I spend on the flowers I could go buy enough garlic to clear the sinus of the whole Italian army. This does not even consider the pain that I get in the back before I am finish and the linimint I got to buy to cure it. Maybe when you get chance you write to you Mamma tell her that its the new style in America to plant the vegatable in the front yard. Specially the garlic, but no mention the fake flower or she get suspizus.

Until then I will remain,

Your Uncle Ambrogio

*I am all exhausted.

Dear Gina,

You stop me if I have tell you this already. Al is come over to visit you Mother one day. She is sit on front porch watch him arive, and as he is coming round the block he get out of the car and push it up to the house. She laff like hell and I no know why, so Al he is tell me. When he is 18 and have his first car he drive her to the store and she is so nervus all the way she drive him crazy with the instrution. She say "Here's a red light." She say "Watch out for the big truck." She say "You go too fast." He no say nothing all this time. All of sudden he is turn off ignition, the car she slows down and he is step out and push and steer at the same time and holler to her "Am I go too fast for you?" You think maybe this would shut her up to be back seat driver but she no quit. They come to railroad station by the traks and she's holler "Make sure no train is come, make sure no train is come." So he is stop in the middle of the traks, get out of the car, put hands over his eyes to block the sun, and is turn very slowly in each direction to look up and down the traks while she is sit in the car scream. She no back seat drive on him no more. She also no get in the car with him if she can help it. She no drive with me either so much for which I feel very fortunate because I go out four five times a day run to the store, run to the gas station, run here, run there, run everywhere. Now I go run to mail this letter.

With lots love, I remain,

Your Uncle Ambrogio

Dear Gina,

I know I have only write you yesterday with the car driving story bout your brother. It have put in my mind another one and I tell it to you now. Albert he take us to visit one of his friend who have beautiful lodge high up in moundain. We have wounderful day, wounderful dinner, wounderful time and when comes time to leave is dark and fug and there we are high on this moundain. In the car we are Albert driving, you Mother next to him and in the beck seat is his wife, you sister Gee Gee and me. Is so dark and so fuggy we are all scare like hell and la paura ci fece rizzare i capelli.* Al he is drive very slowly and follow the lights of car right in front of him, and is follow close by car right beck of us. Al's wife she is so scare she is say to him over and over "I think you on the rong side of the road." He say "No, I'm not." She say "Honey I'm sure you on rong side of road." He say "No, I'm not." Pretty soon they are both talk with their teeth together and the voice they are getting stronger and stronger say Yes you are, No I'm not. Alla fine gli monto la mosca al naso.† All of sudden Al he is slow down and stop the car, forcing the car behind us to stop also. He is get out and go back to the car and return with a stranger. He is say to the man "Sir I would like you to meet my family, I have here my Mother, my Uncle, my wife and my sister." We don't know what the hell he is doing but we say How do you do any way. He then say to the man, "Tell me sir, am I driving on the right side of the road?" The man he say "Yes you are." Al he say "Thank you very much sir" and then he look on his wife and say "Now will you keep your mouth shut" and he get in the car and we drive away. She keep her mouth shut and now I shut mine.

Uncle Ambrogio

*Fear made our hair stand on end.
†Finally he lost his patience.

Dear Gina,

Happy Holloween to you from all the spook here. Noni have me fry the doughnuts all day for the kids who come to the door. She also make me fry the holes. She say the kids they like the round holes better than the doughnuts and she is right again. All the holes they went first and I'm sitting here with few doughnut left. You sister Gee Gee come with her boy friend Bob and they figure to play joke on us. Bob he has on big false nose and glass on his eyes and he put his face by the window in the kitchen to scare you Mother. She look up and see him and she say "Hello Bob — why you no wearin mask tonight?" Then she look on Gee Gee and scream and Gee Gee she is not wear any mask. Gee Gee she jump a foot and Noni polagize for scare her. Then Noni she say "We are too old to make jack-lantern so why you two don't sit in the window for us for while?" Then she click her false teeth out and make Gee Gee jump again. I think it a good thing they take a joke or we don't see them again til maybe next Holloween.

I remember the year you was live in the little house in the back and you have the real long hair and you wash it on Holloween night and while was drying you took broom to sweep the mess the kids make on the porch. You notice we have leave the light on in front so you come run down the strit with broom in you hands to let us know and a man is come around the corner and bump into you and hes let out a yell to see the witch running down the strit with the broom in hands, and he duk across the strit fast as he can and no look back. You don't realize at first why you scare him so bad then you realize it is Holloween night and you sit on our steps and laugh for 20 minits before you can get up and go home. That kind joke only happen once in lifetime and you were lucky one that time.

I say goodby now to the witch with happy reminder that it is time to go Christmas shop.

I remain,

Your Uncle Ambrogio

Dear Gina,

I send hello to you from the Grantz family who are visit us on Sunday for whole day. Seem longer because they have four children but we have nice time thinking and telling old times. We recall Vince and his family if you remember them. Vince he was play the big Hamond organ. You remember how you Mother love to sit listen to him and watch him play? Well we are telling Mr. Grantz about Vince and you Mother she is say to him, "You no see nothing til you see Vince play with his organs." I think Gee Gee she fall through the floor, but nobody say nothing and nobody laugh. You sister she look at me and we decide to let it rest right there like it is. We think it is better to let Mr. Grantz think Vince is little strenge than to hurt you Mother feeling by corret her in front of people. Then Gee Gee she remember the time we are on piknik with Vince and his family at the park. We are sit at piknik tabel with Vince on one end and his son on the other end and Vince holler to the boy, "Hey, Jimmy, throw me the salt" and his boy pick up the salt and throw it and hit Vince between the eye and split his head. Was not so funny then because it spoil everyone lunch, but is funny now. Also the time Vince wife is try to tell us how cat mess all over the house and she is being careful with her words and saying "He oomp on the bed and he oomp on the rug" and her little one he pipe up "Yeah, he crap all over the house" and she hit him on the head with broom handel to shut him up. We have many good laughs and I pass them on to you since you could not be here to enjoy it with you own ears. I also pass on to you beeg kees til next time. Resposto pronto.

I remain,

Your Uncle Ambrogio

Dear Gina,

I am sitting by the dine room tabel to write you because in the kitchen is one big mess like you never see before. A friend of you Mother she come over this morning to bake something for her. She is kind of stuck up woman and she talk to you Mother like she is big dummie. You remember how you Mother used to cook and bake? She would spend a few hour in the kitchen and have the big buffet cover with cookie in no time and enuf food for army. This woman she come and fool around all day with mess all over the place all the time thinking she is showing you Mother something wounderful. After many hours she has produce a small platter with few denty cream puf on it and the kitchen look like somebody had big fight in there. She leave the mess and you Mother and me we are sittin here with the plate of denty cream pufs and the big mess when Gee Gee come in and she say "What happen?" and you Mother she say "Mabel have come over to show me how to make nothing out of something." Gee Gee is in the kitchen now clean the mess and I don't expect to see her for several days and nights. In the meantime we hate to eat the cream pufs because then we will have nothing at all to show for a day as messy as this one. Now you Mother she say Mabel she mean well, but I notice she have rosary in her hands so God must have give her little push to say that. If she was on her own she throw Mabel out the window. The high one in the dining room where I am writing this because I can't go in the kitchen because of the big mess. Next time Mabel come I hide the rosary and we see what happen then. Now I go help Gee Gee out, so you may not hear from me for several days and night. Till then I remain,

Your Uncle Ambrogio

Dear Gina,

Today I find package with two of Rose's teeth in it. Was something she send to you when she was in New York because I find note with it that say, "Dear Gene, you always said you wish you had my teeth, so I am sending you a couple." You Mother and me we laugh like crazy, and I save them in case you still want them so let me know and I send them. Some sisters give the shirt off their back. Yours she give the teeth out of her mouth. I gonna finish clean out the boxes in the closet tomorrow and maybe I find some more interesting things in there. I also find pomes you and Rose write to each other at the dine room table when you was lil kids. I put them on another page and send them with this letter. Noni want to keep this one to have around and hear it once in a while when I read it to her. Bring back memories for her, some for laughing and some for crying, and both kinds to be enjoy. I find picture of the little goat we had in Illinois that you brother use to give the beer to and get him drunk. That goat he love the beer. He would lap it up and then jump round like crazy and come down on his knees. You and Rose use to cry because you think was mean, but I tell you then and I tell you now I never saw a goat have such good time. He always have smile on his face.

I also find the graduation program when you make spich, and if you want I send it. Is called "Pathway to Understanding" and you could give the same spich today under new name "No Communication". (I have heck of a time to spell that one, but it look good to me.) I get busy now print the pomes for you and you kids to enjoy.

Adio,

Uncle Ambrogio

Here are the pome. The first one you write to Rose who was very skinny at the time and you was mad at her and want to make her upset.

The lost chord is the loveliest
By beauty it is kissed
But the most outstanding chord of all
Is the one in Rose's wrist.

This one is about apple core on table. Remember how you pass this pome back and forth?

Rose to Gina

It lies there all unwanted
It tis of use no more
I'm speaking of that withered, brown and curling apple core.

Gina to Rose

It is not right for you to say
Tis of no use in any way
For that brown apple core you see
May someday be an apple tree.

I think this is pretty good consider you were kind of young kids. I think in Junior High School maybe. Show them to Wendy and Lori so you prove how smart you were once. What happen since? (That's a joke.)

Love,

Uncle Ambrogio

Dear Gina,

This morning when Noni get up she say "Thank God it is a nice day today." At breakfast she say, "Thank God for the food." We go sit in the living room and she say "Thank God the TV she works all right." I put the turkey in the oven and she say "Thank God it is a beautiful bird." You brother Al and his wife come in and she say "Thank God you car don't break down." Finally I ask her what all the thank Gods for and she say, "Its Thanksgiving Day and I gotta thank Him for something don't I? Sound funny if I say Thank you for my cancer and diabetes and arthritis, so I thank Him for all the other things I got good." So I say, "I gotta few things to thank Him for too, but how He's gonna hear me when you keep Him busy listen to you all day?" She look up on the ceiling and she say one more, "Thank God for not make me as stupid as Ambrogio."

Al he remind her of the Thanksgiving Day when he was 18 years old and she is talking a lot at the tabel and he say "Shut up Ma" for joke. She just keep talking and again he say "Shut up Ma." And she say "Make me" and he say "I gonna push this pie in you face" and she is stick her nose in his face and say "I dare you" and he take the pumpkin pie very gentel and press into her face and give a few turns and the pumpkin is in her eyes and her nose and she no move a mussel. He sit and look at her while she whipe her face very slowly, then she push back the chair and start to get up and he run fast like anything and she start to chase him. She weigh a lot then, but she catch him just the same and drag him to the tabel and push his face in the butter dish and rub all over his head. We were all watch this show when the neighbor come in to say Happy Thanksgiving and Al is sitting with butter all over his hair and Noni is sitting with pumpkin all over her, and nobody explain why. The neighbor they sit and have coffee and we talk and smile and visit just as if everything is normal and fine.

The smashed pie is in the middle of the tabel next to the mess up butter dish. Noni bring out a fresh pie and we all have dessert together. When she ask them would they like piece pie I wonder if they wonder how she mean. Today Al he rub a little pie on her nose for old times sake, and this time she smile on him. Make a lump in the throat that she can't chase him any more.

Now I say Thank God we are all here this day, and you are all well and content. Maybe next year we can say Thank God you are here with us for Thanksgiving dinner.

A kees for everybody.
Con amore,*

Uncle Ambrogio

*With love

Dear Gina,

Are you still smokin cigaretes? I watch the TV bout it and make me crazy. First they show man walk long way for cigaret, then nother time they show man stagger and coff from it. Even the people they don't smoke could have nervouse break down watch this. When you sister Yola start to smoke when she was young you Mother tell her all these same things they show on TV now. First time she catch Yola smoke she was in basement standing in front of the furnace with the door open blow the smoke in. Noni is stand behind her watchin for long time. When she catch you you were sitting by open window blow the smoke out. When she catch Al he was hidin in the garage blow the smoke all over the place because he was not worry bout getting caught. When she catch Gee Gee she was in the bathroom waving the talcum powder all over the place. Now when she watch these guys on TV she say "I know that 30 years ago. What take them so long to catch on?" She never catch Rose because she was to smart to get caught. When she finally get up the nerve she light one in front of Noni and Noni was disappoint because she was wanting to find Rose's hiding place herself.

When Noni go to the doctor for her pills he give her report on her arthritis, her diabetes, her enlarge heart, her cancer condition, her high blood pressure, then he say was good thing she never smoke in her life and Noni say "Bigga deal." The doctor have to laugh himself at how stupid he sound.

Now I stop to go hide in storage house and have smoke.

I remain,

Your Uncle Ambrogio

Dear Gina,

Our neighbor Myrtle she just left here and I think she is running down the block to reach as many people as she can with the gosip she just get from you Mother, and you Mother does not know yet that she gave it. I keep tell her to learn to talk American better or she get in troubel some day and I think this was the day. You know she have lots troubel with words what end in ER — like she can not say butter so instead she say bar — and she also have troubel with words they end in LM so she can not say calm and instead she is say common. Myrtle she is here visiting and they are talking about Claudine who you Mother like very much. She is trying to tell Myrtle how quiet and calm Claudine she is, and how she go from place to place helping and cheering up the people all the time. You Mother call her the butterfly. So she is say to Myrtle, "That Claudine she hop from place to place like barfly and she is very common person." Myrtle her eyes pop open and she say "Really?" and I think now she is hopping from place to place to tell what she hear about Claudine.

It remind me of the time you ask you Mother for dime and she say "Go get it. It is on my dress near the statch by the cloz." And nobody in the room can figure out how you know exactly where to go get that dime, which was near the statue on her dresser which was by the closet. I still got to laugh when I think about it.

When I try to interupt to straiten the thing out today, you Mother say to me "You keep out — who inwite you on this compazation?" I say "You mean conversashun" and she say "That's what I said, stupido." and I drop it right there. There is always possibility that Myrtle does not realize you Mother is talking wrong and maybe think that she is the one who is hearing wrong, but I don't think so. I can no complain about her speakin for a while til she forget how I keep pot of coffee in refrigarator which I tell you about in next lettera because for now I am quiting and remaining

Your Uncle Ambrogio

Dear Gina,

I don't wait to hear from you because I think you maybe going crazy wonder about a pot of coffee in the refrigarator and I'm sorry I ever mengen in my last lettera because is on my mind to explain, which I should have done right away and enjoy my life instead of walk around try to remember to tell you next time which is this time and I can forget it.

I make big pot coffee on the stove and am going to pour cup when you Mother holler from dining room to bring her glass juice. So with one hands I open refrigarator and to take out the juice I set the coffee pot on the shelf just long enough to put the juice on the tabel, and the door she swing shut and I forget the pot is in there. By this time you Mother she come in the kitchen and she say "Where is the coffee pot?" and I remember just as she say it and I answer "In the refrigarator." She say all right and she take it out of refrigarator and she pour a cup for herself and me too. We are sitting drinking and I am thinking about it and getting insult more each minit that she act like it is a natural thing for me to do to put hot coffee pot in refrigarator like I am nuts or something, so I say to her "Why you don't ask me why the pot is in the refrigarator like I am nuts or something?" and she say "It's a free country, you can put the pot where ever you want" and I still don't know if she is laughing inside or not which is really drive me crazy in my mind in the end. I think I may test her out and put the pot in there every morning and see how long she last with the smart alek way she got about it. If her girls they take after her all their husband they die young from too much woundering.

I hope you are happy that you finally got the story bout the pot because I am feeling very good bout it myself that it is over with. I rest now and remain,

Uncle Boo

Dear Gina,

I hate to let you know this news that you have crazy relatives here in this part of the country. Don't feel worry about it. You are far enuf away and maybe didn't catch it from anybody. Besides all the nuts in the house, we have big tree in the front with the walnuts. The darn squirrel from across the strit they come each day and take away one at a time. I decide to set trap for them so I make fancy one—a box with lid that raise up with snap on it to close fast. I want to know right away when I catch him so I put string on the trap door, run it across the yard to front porch, thru the front door, across the dining room, around the corner into the kitchen and tie to a glass milk bottle in the sink. So now as soon as that trap door she snap shut the string will pull and the bottle she will fall over in the sink and I will know I catch the squirrel. This trap is sitting like this for several weeks and during this time you sisters and brother they come in and out to visit many times. They duk under this string, they push it out of their way, they are careful not to shut the door on it, and not one time do any of them ask what the string is. Is just as bad as the coffee pot in the refrigarator. If you come in a house and you see a crazy string that go everywhere you look, don't you think to ask what is this crazy string go all over the house? Nobody ask. I wait and wait and nobody ask. They just keep duking and pushing, go under, go round, and don't ask. I have decide that even if I catch all the squirrel tomorrow, I leave this string here til somebody ask what it is. Until then,

I remain,

Your Uncle Ambrogio

Dear Gina,

I wake up this morning and find bunch broken glass in sink where the bottle crash. I run outside to look at the trap and I find cat inside. I take the string down right away and hope nobody remember it to ask what was it. You Mother she holler like crazy about the glass in the sink and the squirrel they still runnin back and forth with the other nuts. If I knew which tree they live in I carry them all over for them in one trip and spoil all the fun. They make me crazy.

I remain you crazy uncle,

Ambrogio

Dear Gina,

You brother come over this morning soon after I write to you and when he is walk in, first thing he say is "Where is the string?" I say "What string?" and he say "The one you tie on you milk bottle so nobody can steal it." I thought you like to know that.

Love and kees,
Uncle Ambrogio

Dear Gina,

Thank you very much for the beautiful Christmas presants what you send to all of us. You are good Sanda Claus. This year as special presant I give everyone big joke on myself that last them many years. I am look at the tag on the presant you send which say "To Boo" and the B she is look like a 3 and confuse me and I say "Whats this 300?" and the family they all laff like crazy and never let me forget now. So next year I don't give them anything because I give them joke they can enjoy every Christmas. Was bad enuf when little girl next door see your letter that say "Dear Zio"* and she look on the Zio and she say "What does 210 mean?" Now I put them together and I am call 510 but only to my relative and close friends.

Gee Gee she give me ukelele to play but is not so easy to do yet. Remind me of the mandolin in the old country which was mostly playd under somebodys window at night. When Noni was young girl the boys they sing under the window every night. Her Father have to bring extra water from the well so he have some for drink, some for wash and clean and some for throw out the window on their head to shut them up. (I read this to you Mother and she say now I start callin her Noni like the kids and pretty soon she dont remember what her name is any more.) (I tell her "You call me Stupido for so many years I dont remember my name so good already" and she say "You name is 300, Stupido.")

*Dear Uncle

Everybody come for Christmas dinner and Noni she look around the table for one Dago and cant find one. Her kids all mary to Irish, French, German and Polish. She look around and say "Welcome to the League of Nation". We miss you very much speciale since Russia was not represent without you.

Happy New Year during which I remain,

Your Uncle 510

Dear Gina,

You sister Rose she is visiting with me and you Mother today and she is paint her nails at the dine room table. The color she put is not so dark as the one I wear once, and in case you woundering what I'm saying, I tell you.

When you lil sister Gee Gee she is 6 years old, I am dozing to sleep and she come to me and ask me can she paint my nails. I am so sleepy I no pay much tention to what she say and I just say yes and I go to sleep. Next morning I get up and hurry to get ready to catch the train for work and I see my nails they are all paint bright red and I got no time to do nothing bout it. I keep my hands in my pocks lots til I get on the train, then I hide in back and try to scretch that darn stuff off and I see guy he is watching me. I feel like dam fool, but I just keep scratchin fast as I can. Good thing he not look like the sweet type or I'm in lots troubel. I no ball Gee Gee out for this because if I do them cow eyes of hers fill up with tears. She have excess water storage there in the best of condition anyway, and she make them lil lips like cow catcher on train when she get ready to cry. Those are the times when she is so upset she say to me, "I love you but I no like you."

Nother time I am take her for walk and she run ahead me and find something on the sidewalk and she come run back so happy hollering "Look — I find pack balloons," and she is ready to blow one up. You know what kind balloons she find in nice neat package all white and roll flat. She is so happy I have hell of a time to get it away from her, but I manage it by take her to get some real balloons in bright color, hoping we don't meet anyone long the way. Scusa this dirty story.

I remain,

Your Uncle Ambrogio

Dear Gina,

My friend and neighbor Tony from down the strit come by today to return to me a Get Well card I send him which he did not deserve. Happen like this. He call me one day to tell me he have take out the car and smash it up pretty good. His wife is so mad on him she no talk to him, she no feed him, and she no let him go out of house. He say to me, "I am here in bondage" and I think he say bandage and I send him Get Well card. So today he bring it back and I save it for a time when he really need it.

He have on his overcoat which he wear all year round because he is so proud of it since he came from Italy and buy it. I am sittin sweatin and he is sittin proud in his coat. The poor guy is have bad time to buy blankets in the winter, but I'm sure he is not wear it to bed. No make senze to me a guy like this, while at the same time Mrs. President she is redecorate the White House which is already beautyful as is. I wonder what she do with old blankets?

You Mother she come and sit with us for awhile, but she is act so disgust at him for sit there in that coat on summer day, I whisper to her, "No act so disgust" and she say "I'm no acting."

I stop now with big baccione,*

Uncle Ambrogio

*Kiss

Dear Gina,

Noni and I we are sitting wait for the priest to come today. He come every Friday to hear confession and give Comunion, and is also visit with us a little bit. I hope he show up after last week. Maybe hes busy today make arrengments to put us in crazy house. You remember the bull fight poster Gee Gee give me for joke with my name print on the bottom with all the bull fighters? The priest look on that last week and he say, "Hey Ambrogio, I don't know you was bull fighter" and you Mother say "He's not a bull fighter Father — hes big bull thrower." I guess I am lucky at that when I think what she could say at the time, which I am sure she think of it but she don't say it because she was deal with a priest.

Remind me of time in the hospital the night before her operation when the priest come in to hear her confession and give comunion in case she doesn't make it and she tell him she has already have both, so he tell her "That's all right, and you don't have to worry anyway because I know whenever it is you get to the gate they gonna open it for you" and she say "You goddam right Father" and his eye glass slide down on his nose and he almost fall off the chair. Then he say "Now you did it. Now you got to have confession all over again" and she say "Thats all right, was worth to see the look on you face." So I got to leave the room while he hear her confess, which I was glad to do because I want to get out of there anyway. Then I go back in and I ask her how she feel and she say "If it wasn't for my body I would feel wounderful", so what are you gonna do with somebody like that I'm ask you. I ask her is she sure she want operation and she say "Bird in the hands could make a big mess and rolling stone no catch you if you run fast enough." She leave me strand with that and I tell her maybe I am too stupid to understand her proverb and she say "If the shoe fit, go to Hell." Then she laugh to cheer me up little bit but it is too late. When she wake up the next day from operation she say "You still here stupido?" but I am so glad she is still here that I don't say nothing.

When the nurse come in she doesn't know you Mother she is still very sharp and no dummie, so she is talking right in to her face like she is half deaf and a lot stupid. She is call her Mama and she is holler in her eyes, "You be fine Mama," and I feel so bad to see someone treat her like she is child and I want to cheer her up, so after the nurse she is gone I say, "No pay no attention to that dummie nurse the way she talk" and you Mother say, "Don't be hard on them — they work so hard. You see how young that one is and she's deaf already."

When I am visit her later in the week we hear man cross the hall moan and moan and I say "Whats happen to him?" and she say "The poor man hes run under a truck." I laugh to myself and I think I gotta remember to tell Gina that one.

Now my hands shes tired from all this writing so I hang up now with big baccione to everyone. Resposto pronto.

I remain,

Your Uncle Ambrogio

Dear Gina,

Now she's the time for all good men to come to the aid of his country. I learn that today and sound like heck of a good idea. What a crazy place this is I can't believe it most of time. My car is park in front of the house face the wrong way, which at the time I did not know was the wrong way. There are bunch of ruff neck kids around it act crazy, yelling, screaming, no shoes and sloppy. Comes a polisman and I think "Good, he is chase that gang away." Instead he is go past them and come to me to bawl me out for park the car face the wrong way. I say to him "Whats the difference what way it face? Them kids probly steal it as soon as you gone." What a crazy place. It's too bad them kids don't have place to go pick figs to keep busy.

I am lookin for copy of pome I remember from long time ago call "The Ballad of the Harp Weaver" which I like very much. I apreciate if you can find this for me as I am lookin for long time. Is story of Mother who is poor and she weave the clothes for her kids on harp strings, and in the morning they find her dead with hands in harp strings and pile of clothes beside her. Is beautiful pome and I hope you can find it for me.

I am back with my Breed Frensh Speller and I go out of my way to make confusion for myself. I find made and maid. I find blue and blew. I find steak and stake. I find through and threw. I find brake and break. I wish I was back with to, too and two. I gonne be plenty blue before I am through, so I stop and take a break and eat big steak. Took me whole hour to write that last line. And that is the trouth.

> Adio.
> I remain,
>
> Your Uncle Ambrogio

Dear Gina,

Buon giorno! This is crazy way to start lettera because is afternon, but I do it anyway. I try to bake some things this morning with you Mother tellin me what to do, and I half to be scientist to figure out what the heck she is talking about. She no measure nothing. She say "Put handsfull this and handsfull that" like I really know what she is saying. Then she say "Mix all together till it feels right." Continues to feel wrong to me because I don't know how it suppose to feel when it feel right. Then she say "Roll out on the board til looks right." When comes out rong she call me stupido and I agree with her because if I wasn't I would not be there in the first place. Or the second place or the third place. And that's the way it is around this place. All day I'm singing song I used to sing to you and Rose when you were little babys. "Long time ago, Gina and Ro Ro, coma froma Italy to maka soma dough." That has nothing to do with bake the cookie, but I was do both things at same time — sing the song and ruin the cookie. Now I ruin the English little bit and I'm threw for the day. So you answer me just the same and I send to you big baccione, and say arrividerci, hasta manana, half a banana and Pepsi Cola.

Resposto Pronto.

Uncle Ambrogio Bruno Boo 300 210 = 510

Dear Gina,

Last night we have family get together and miss you very much. To make you feel better about it, you no miss very much. Why is because I make mistake to bring out the wine and you brother make mistake to drink too much. Would be all right cept the people next door are visiting us with friend of theirs who dont know us at all. This is the first impreshun they get. You brother Al he's get drunk, he's talk too loud and show off a little bit and the stranger lady say to you Mother "Is that you son?" and Noni she say "Not right now he's not." Her smart alek mood is continue today when I say to her "I go on the market, you want something?" and she say "Not after you go on it I don't." She have got very bitter lips today but they gonna sweetin up as soon as something good pass thru. Plendy have pass thru last Sunday when we are have spaghetti dinner and I see she is eat too much. I make the mistake of say to her "You eat too much" and she say "I only have one fork full", and I say "Yeah, but is pitchfork." And that's how I ruin the rest of the week for myself. Now arent you glad you not here?

I remain,

Your Uncle Ambrogio

Dear Gina,

I look throu the picture album and come cross picture of one uncle of mine that I send you. He's the one I told you when we ask him how old he is he say "I'm 81 or 87 — I don't know which one but I'm sure it was in the winter." I want you to see him what he looks like after I tell you that story so many time. I didn't even know I had it and I'm not positive it is him. Now I sound like he does, but I think maybe it is him. In fact I'm sure it is him. You send it back after you see it and til then I remain,

Your Uncle Ambrogio

P.S. I really am not so sure it is him. Just say that for peace of mind.

Kees

Dear Gina,

Yesterday you Mother and I we have nice visit with Gee Gee in her nice apartament. Getting there was easy but coming back was not so good. She fix us nice early dinner at 3 o clock so we have plenty time for nice chitchat. However you Mamma she's afraid she gonna ride home in the dark so by 4 oclock she's naggin me "Lets go, lets go." I argue with her theres no hurry, we only got to go six block, but she still keeps naggin "Lets go, lets go before gets dark out." My situation worsen when she starts to rain outside so now you Mamma is nag "Lets go before the tunter and lightning she start." What the hell, I finally give up and we leave. By the time we reach home was rain pretty good and I have umbrela in back seat. She is get out and hollering to me "No forget the umbrela, no forget the umbrela", so I grap it, put it over my head and walk in the house and she is left standing outside getting wet and holler a lot. I feel bad about my little joke so I run back out to get her and forget the umbrela and we both get wet. To patch it up completly, today I present her with little gift. I find a cane in storage house in back which she can use to make easier for her to walk. I have also place a weapon in her hands.

Adio.

Your dumb Uncle Ambrogio

Dear Gina,

I get so mad on you Mother I gonna tattle on her to you so I get it off my chest. I am very worry if she don't take her pills when she suppose to so I try to put across to her how important is for her to take them when she should. I talk to her for hour. I tell her how better she feel for taking them, how the doctor depend on her to behave herself, how she got to eat right and take the right pill at the right time. I talk and talk and she listen and listen and I think I am getting somewhere and I get all finish and she look at me and she say "Bool sheet." So what I'm gonna do with her I'm askin you? I buy the diet ice cream because she should not have the rich kind, but I put in regular carton so she don't know and I feed it to her every day til it is gone. When it's all finish she say "That was terrible and how long it take you to put it in the rong box?" What make me the most mad is I cant keep from laugh when at the same time I want punch her in the nose so bad. Also at the same time I wish I could feed her all the good stuff she love, poor thing. She has trubel watch the TV now because it bother her eyes, and most time she just sit and look out the window with rosary in her hands. But she don't complain and so I don't either. She was so happy when you call from Los Angeles, and she say "Thanks God for Frankaleen Benjaleen" and I say "Why?" and she say "Don't he invent the telephone?" and I say, "Oh, yeah" so she don't feel stupid, and now I hope she never happen to see that movie with Don Ameche in it. She will tell me how stupid I am and if she does I won't have argument.

I remain,

Your Uncle Ambrogio

Dear Gina,

You brother Al and his wife were visit us this afternoon and Noni she was dying to tell some story on him
when he was young, and Al he keep stopping her to keep
himself out of trubel. So I tell you one and you no tell him I
tell you. When he is 19 years old he bring home woman he
want to marry who is 39 and have son 10 year old. You
Mother she is upset bout that but she know if she say
something to him then he marry her for sure. So she invite
the woman to dinner and she is very polite and nice to her
all the time that Al is sit at the tabel. She is smile and be
sweet and keep push food in her. Then she send Al on
errand and when he leave the room she still smile and say
to the woman "My son no need nother Mother. You marry
him and I break you head." And she keep eatin and smilin.
The woman she disapear forever and Al he still don't
know why. Only I know why and now you know.

She keep him out lots trubel that way when he was
young, but she don't baby him too much neither. Many
times he come in to complain that somebody pick on him
and she say "The tree no shake if the wind no blow."
Which is true. And what she didn't fix with a few words
she use shotgun. We have corn field many years ago in the
old house in Illinois and we know somebody is stealing the
corn every night from it. One night Noni take shotgun and
sit by the bedroom window which face the field. She sit in
the dark for long time and pretty soon comes somebody
thru the field stealing the corn. She raise the window very
quiet and aim the gun and she holler "I give you three to
get out my yard!" and she yell fast "One two three!" and
she shoot. Next day she see Mr. Ball from across the strit

walk funny like he has buckshot in his pants and she smile and wave to him and say "Oh, so it was you Mr. Ball." And she smile thru that too. He have a time to figure out why the smile on her face does not match the pain in his behind. And now I got pain in my hands so I stop.

Resposto pronto,

Uncle Ambrogio

Dear Gina,

Very delight to get you letter and to hear that Gary he comes to visiting often and does good in school. It shure relieve my mind a lot that he is able to do these things after he hurt his eye so bad. It is too bad you don't have picture of him on pony when he was little. They don't take picture of kid on pony any more like they use to do. There was time you could not look thru picture book without come cross at least one kid on pony. Now he is too big to put on pony. Besides his wife will think he is crazy. Maybe they don't make the pony any more. Come to think about it, I don't see one for long time anyplace. I don't mean regular pony because I realize that every horse was once a pony. I mean the pony what never get bigger. You know what I'm talkin bout? Is something to ponder. This is new word I pick up lately. It mean to think over something. How come it sound so much like thunder and spelled different? I still am going crazy with these spell words. I got the book to learn called Breeds French Speller. It has English words in it so why is call French speller? I don't figure out. They go out of there way to do thing the hard way in this country. I see the words boot and foot spell alike and pronounce two way. The foot sound like put and the boot sound like lute which also sound like toot. And high sound like bye and that's what I do now — say bye.

Love and keeses,
Uncle Ambrogio

Dear Gina,

We are having one beautiful morning here. This is not true. It is rain like crazy but who want to start lettera out with such a gloom news? So we are having one beautiful morning here. The sun she is shining. We just can not see it on account of the rain. I tell Noni "When it is finish the world she be nice and clean" and she say "How you gonna know when you never wipe you eye glass?" I pause now to wipe my eye glass. I tell her she have no poetry in her soul and she tell me if I no shut up my face I no have no food on my plate. I play it smart so now not only will I have food on my plate but I will be able to see what it is I'm eatin.

Right now we are having some cracker with cheese on it and she is holding the dish and I say "I have one too" and she say "Make up you mind." Now I have to decide is it worth to explain to her about to too and two and I decide no mainly because I'm still not so sure about it myself. Instead I put on the TV to keep her mind busy with them soap opra which drive me nuts sometimes. She is so worry about them people — she cry when they cry and she get mad at the bad ones and she talk back to them. Is not as bad as when she use to watch the rassler. She broke several ash tray stand slamming them on the floor trying to help the good guy all she can. Was good to hear her call somebody else stupido for a change. I miss them guys.

You know how she pronounce Tuesday and Thursday both the same. She call them both Thuesday. I ask her "When the visiting nurse come again?" and she say "Thuesday." I say "Do you mean Tuesday or Thursday?" and she say "The one next to Wednesday, Stupido." Makes me happy I don't take a chance on too and to and two.

With a big baccione I remain,

Your Uncle Ambrogio

Dear Gina,

    I no like complain bout this country, but sometimes I got to get things off my chest or start revlution. This driver licenze business is drive me crazy. I study the book for many weeks, and Al gives me the test what he take to look on. I say to myself "I study the book so I know all the answer, and I drive in this country for 50 years, so why I worry? I just put in my mind all the check marks on Al's test and I learn them by heart down the row and I go for my licenze." You know them guys they change the test and give me nother one and almost all my marks they are wrong? I go back again, and I take lots time to get it right, but the way they have them words twist round such a sneaky way, I no make it second time. By now the man there is call me by my first name. When I walk in he's holler "Hello Bruno!" I think maybe I should make good friends with him and if he don't give me dam licenze then he can drive me where I want to go every day. I go back third time and I say to him "Forget them test — you come get in the car with me and I show you I drive good" and he do it. He ask me all kind question as we go, and he take me round and round and make me park and turn and pretty soon he say "O.K. you drive fine and you get you licenze." Now I got to worry for 4 years and hope he is still there when I go back for nother one. In the meantime I give Al back his test paper and give him letcher on how it no pay to cheat. He should know better in the first place.

                I remain,

                Your Uncle Ambrogio

Dear Gina,

I got picture for you to put in you mind which is funny one, so you concatret and put this picture. You Mother and me we are sittin watching TV and the doorbell she ring. You Mother she answer the door and who is standing there but you Pop. You realize they have not see each other since divorce many years ago. She look on him like she just see him yesterday and she say "Yes, what you want?" He say "I come to see the kids, but my wife she is wait in the car." Now you realize if this was in Italy or even here many years ago you Mother she have slam the door long ago. However she have learn lots watchin the TV and she handle situation very smooth. She say "Tell the poor thing to come in." So Pop he bring the poor thing in and Mama she say to her "Here, sit in the soft chair, you poor thing." You lil sister Gee Gee she is laughing til crying in the corner because she know what Noni mean, and I know what Noni mean, but the poor thing she doesn't. The poor thing she says "We have terrible time driving over the moundain and we almost went over one time, but we didn't." Noni she say "That's too bad." Then the poor thing say, "I can hardly sit down" and Noni say "Yes, I know." Also, the poor thing she have lot hair on her face which she evidantli have try to shave, so she have beard shadow, and Noni say to Gee Gee "Say hello to you Father. He is the one in the pants." I don't know if Pop catch on to this business going on, but if he does then he is a good sport because he not give anything away, but just smile lots. When they leave Noni help the poor thing to the door and say "Be careful you not fall down my steps, you got enuff truble already." I hope you enjoy this picture in you mind because you soon see the real thing since they are on their way to see you. Try to wipe the picture out while they are there and make one of your own.

I remain,

Your Uncle Ambrogio

Dear Gina,

Noni want to know do you have picture of Gee Gee when she was little girl in dance recite in the costume. She look all over and can't find one. You was pretty small also (means too) at the time so I don't know if you remember the show or not. Gee Gee she have long beautiful curls then and her little girl friend have long blond curls. The teacher put them next to each other in the middle of the other girls on the stage. The other little girl she is named Judy and her Mother is sit in back of us. Pretty soon her Mother lean over and say to us "My Judy certainly stands out" and Noni she say "Thats because she is next to the prettiest one up there" which shut her up good. Sometime Noni have tongue so sharp I dont know how she dont cut herself when she lick her lips. If you have the picture you send it fast so she quits nag me to look for something we have not got.

She find you first grade picture and she talk about the time the boys was put snake down Yola's back. Noni go to the school and tell the teacher she want to see their Mother. The teacher she arrange a meeting but make Noni promise she dont say nothing nasty to the woman. You Mother she walk into the meeting and punch her good one and then say to the teacher, "See, I no say one bad words" and out she go. When the woman recover they become good friends. Yola no get no more snake down her back. One of the boy is in picture with you in first grade and we point to him and say "There is the one with the snakes" and then we got to explain what we are talking bout to who ever is unlucky to be present at the time. I stop now so you can quit reading and go look for the picture.

I remain,

Your Uncle Ambrogio

Dear Gina,

Noni she just say to me "Are you write to my door?" I say "No, I'm writing to your window." Right away I'm in trubel. Then I spend hour try to teach her to say daughter but she just can't say ER no matter how hard she try. She say "I want some war" and I say "Go to Vietnam, they got plenty there." Then I'm in trubel again. But I have lots fun pass my time this way and I wait for my chance lots of times to catch her. I ask how Claudine is feeling and Noni say "She's bare" and I say "No, she got her clothes on." One time she and Mrs. Neggi talk to each other for half hour and neither one know what the other is sayin but they keep right on going. Mrs. Neggi she talk with strong German accent. She look up to the sky and say "Where the sun is this morning?" and Noni say "He's work on the gas station like usual." Sometimes I shake my head and walk away and I don't say nothing because they are enjoy each other just as much as if they knew what they are saying. Who am I to spoil it?

This morning I want to cheer her up so I go outside and pick three leafs clover and spend half hour sticking extra leaf on it and I bring it to her and say "Look, I find you four leafs clover" and she say "What for?" I say "For good luck" and she say "If my luck was good would take you longer to find it so you leave me alone for awhile." But she take it just the same. Tomorrow I might find it on my dish for breakfast.

I have decide to take up drawing and am makeing pictures of birds and flowers which I will send you some for your opinion. It is not necessary for you to be honest.

I remain,

Your Uncle Ambrogio

Dear Gina,

You Mother and I we sit and watch Lassie on the TV tonight and I never see dog like this. They don't got this kind in the old country I know for sure. We have not decide if the dog is very smart or the people they are very stupid. Then we think it must be the people who are watch that are maybe very stupid. This man in the story is trap and he say to the dog "Go to the truck and get me piece of rope" and the dog he run right to the truck and he get it. I'm surprise the dog he doesn't say "You want hemp or nylon, and how long a piece you want?" You Mother she figure they got piece of raw meat in that truck under the rope to make him run there in the first place. I realize they got to do the sneaky things like that, but at the same time they make jackass out of the people who are watchin the dog, don't they? I say to Skippy one time "Go get me the paper" and he run out and no show up for three days. That's the kind dog they should have on TV, one you can believe what you see. Of course in that case the man in the truck he dies but at least you could believe it. Still is not as bad as Flipper.

We got cat next door who is very smart. The one I catch in my string trap one time. He still like me just the same because he know was an accident, and he is very smart cat. Of course I never send him after rope yet. But he is come runnin every morning when he hear me at back door and we always have few words to say to each other. This is pretty crazy letter and I shut up now with love from

Pretty crazy Uncle Ambrogio

Dear Gina,

What you think about purple paint for kitchen walls?
Please answer right away.

Adio,

Uncle Ambrogio

Dear Gina,

You smash me a good one with your answer. I have porch full of cans left over paint with not enuf of one color for the kitchen so I gonna be smart and mix them all together. They come out purple and Noni she look and she say "You not gonna paint my kitchen purple." I say "Purple she is beautiful color." She say "Purple is ugly color." I say "I gonna paint it." She say "You not gonna paint it." I say "I write ask Gina should I paint it and she settle the argument." Now that you settle the whole thing you can tell me where I'm gonna dump three gallons purple paint. I send them C.O.D. in case you change you mind bout the color purple.

I remain,

Your Uncle Ambrogio

Dear Gina,

I am having glass home made wine which remind me of time of prohibition when we use to make it in the basement. Noni she had the little neighborhood grocery store at the time and once in while she sell bottle under the counter. One day polis they come to search the place because they have hear bout it. Noni was then much heavier than even now and wear long dress. When she see them come in store she sit on wine barrel and cover it, then she tell them what wounderful job they do to protect the people, and to help themself look the place over. She sit there long time giving the spich while they search and no find nothing. Before they go they polagize for bother her and she tell them she is glad they are doing such good job. Whenever I have glass home made wine I remember those days. We had to put the barrel in different place to not worry bout it and not sell any for while til whole thing blows over.

She had lots courage then like she has now. She didn't know many English words and she doesn't want to talk Italian when she get to this country in order to learn. She had lots help from the neighbors when they come to the store. They make their own change and I'm sure no one ever cheat her of a penny. To this day she is still not saying colonder — she call it "Spaghetti stay, water go" and she say the colonder is something to see what day it is. She refuse to say scola pasta, also, in order to talk American. When you kids use to play the game with her of naming lots numbers very fast and she give the correct total right away, then when you do your arithmatic you sit with pencil for hour to add same kind colum of figure and then come up with the rong answer. If she had chance for education I think maybe she be the first President of United States who was not citizen.

It is pleasure for me to write these memorys down like this and is the only good thing bout you being so far away so I have reason to do it.

I remain,

Your Uncle Ambrogio

Dear Gina,

I sit now and look on you Mother empty chair and my hands heavy to write. I know you heart she is the same and I hope you are doin all right while wait for time to recover. I look on all you kids there by her funeral and I think she leave lots of things with you that you will realize little at time in days to come. When she is layin in hospital she know that this time she was not come out but she smile and laugh to the end. You think back how when you come in to the room and hold her hands and she say "I have something to say to you," and she is sound so serious and my heart jump because I think she have give up finally. Then she take you hands in hers and say very serious, "I got lots persimmon in the freezer — don't forget to take some to the kids." What a beautiful woman. Remember what the priest say in church — "If she was sit with us here now she would be think to herself I hope they all have plenty to eat when this darn funeral is over," and that is perfect words to describe her. So try to think that when you feel sad. If you think bout her exactly the way she was, then you gotta smile.

Uncle Ambrogio

Part II

Dear Gina,

Now you are settle back home with Earl and the kids, and I hope that life is like normal once more for you but don't hope for too much that it will ever be like it was before because you must realize that now you live with sadness. However, you find soon that the memory become sweeter and sweeter and avengally take over.

The house is empty and quiet with no one to yell on me, which I use to enjoy and you Momma she know that. I jump in my car and escape with any excuse I find.

I see the boy what use to wave at her by the window each day and he seem to know without ask. He walk on the other side of the street now, but one of these day he come back on this side. That is what you will do in you heart. No watch the clock. Si faccia corragio.*

I love you,

Uncle Ambrogio

*Get up your courage.

Dear Gina,

Albert does not come to the house often and I am thinkin it is difficult for him to come in. He and Noni did not use the words to send love beck and forth, but when they was look on each other the love pour out their eyes and fall on cheecks. She was plendy proud of him and at the same time was worrying when he was boxing and try for Golden Gloves in Chicago. You Pop and me we build him a boxin ring in the basement so he can practise. When it was finish Pop say to him, "Come on, I spar with you lil bit" and Al he say "No, Pop, I don't want to hurt you." Pop say "You be careful and you no hurt me." Al say "No, I'm afraid I hurt you." Pop say "Come on, you no hurt me." So they are get in the ring and Al is dancin around very fancy, with lots of jabbing in the air and Pop he swing once and hit him in the jaw, knock him out. Then Pop he fall on his knees yellin "Bertie, did I hurt you? Pop no mean to hurt you." We throw cold water on Al to bring him round and he got himself new spar partner his own age. We keep that a secret from his friends also. And you no tell him I tole you neither til I tell him first.

I think I better do that now.
Adio,

Uncle Ambrogio

Dear Gina,

Thank you for the packages wrapped goodies which you forgot to put tags on so I know which one is which one. Don't worry bout it — I did the same thing myself once. I came home very proud with big bargen. I say to you Mother, "I got big bargen. Whole bunch canned goods for haf price becaus the labels were off them." She say, "Oh, really? How I know whats inside to plan meal?" I say "You take you chances like grap bag." She took her chances throu 6 cans before she hit the one she want. I ate lots beets which I don't like, and I ate them with smile on my face thru purpol teeth, even for brekfast. Then for few more days I have okra, which I dint even know what it was, and would been happy to put off the introducshun for few more years. I also enjoy several meal of Boston Brown Bread which I wish never leave Boston. Stead of saying "Its time for dinner" she holler "Come and get you bargens." One time she stand in doorway with can in one hands and can opener in other and she stand there for long time til I say "Why you stand there?" and she say, "I enjoy the suspenze." One time Al say to her, "Well anything exciting happen today?" and she say, "Yes, I got peas on the first try." He look in cupboard and say, "Maybe the stuff is hot so they remove identficashun." It was helluva long time before I brout home nother bargen.

I hope this make you feel better bout not labelling which cake have the nuts and which one have the fruit.

I remain,

Your Uncle Ambrogio

Dear Gina,

You see what I find and send to you. Is copy of pome Gary write for me when he is in high school. You make copy for you and sent it back. You see what smart son you got there. Show him and see if he remember this.

Uncle Ambrogio

I Just Doant Understand English:
(A pair-a-dee in poetree)

Are you familiar with the fact
Our English language ain't intact?
It ain't consistent, ain't concise,
Like mouse is mice, but house ain't hice.

Can you explain how it can be
That it doant make no sense to me,
That words aren't spelled the way they sound
And worse the other way around.

Why is a fireplace full of soot?
Which looks and sounds like foot and put,
While put, in golf, comes out like putt,
And there's no extra "T" in nut.

And we say door the same as more,
Then make it worse with poor and pour,
And sure and shoe, like new and knew
Will never look alike to you.

There's blood and hood and mood and brood,
So why not crood and rood and lood?
And if there's gore and lore and shore,
Why mess it up with boar and roar?

If I am cut I'm dripping blud,
And won must swim when in a flud,
Unless you flote upon a bord,
But if it's sharp, you might be gourd.

Why can't I rent a place to lage,
And park my kar in a garodge?
And rest when things have bin kwite tuff,
And press a pleet and foaled a cugh?

And for my favorite players rute,
And flirt with females who are kyoot,
And when I'm naked I am nood,
And if in company, it's rood.

So contemplate where I have rote,
And of my bafflement take noat,
I kood go on with meny moar,
But what's the use? What for, four, fore?

Dear Gina,

Your Uncle Sam come to visit me from Los Angeles. Aunt Phil she couldnt come because she was not feeling well, which I was sorry to hear. He tell me you visit back and forth often with your Cousin Mario and his wife Marilyn, which I was glad to hear.

Do you ever remind Mario of how you use to blame everything on him when he was kid to keep youself out of trubel? When he come for summer vacation one time and you broke the bicycel and Noni say who did it, you say Mario did it. She won't holler at him becaus he was guest in house. However you did it so much she soon catch on, but she don't say nothing. Then one time she throw away the movie star pictures that you save and you went run to her crying bout it and she look you in eyes and say "Mario did it". Do you recall that lesson?

The next time you see them give good regard from me,

Their Uncle Ambrogio

Dear Gina,

I am tired from spending my day make useless attempts to pay my electricity bill. I start out this morning with bill and the money in my hands and I get pretty close when I come to sign what say ONE WAY STREET. This surprise me because never was there before. So I circle round and come up the other side and find another sign what say NO ENTER. I think maybe I attak from the rear, so I go round again in order to come upon another sign say DO NOT ENTER — ONE WAY STREET. After 30 years I don't know why they want make it so difficult for people to pay their bill. I come home disgust, with the bill and the money still in my hands and I am plan to sit here until those guys find out how stupid they are. My signs make more sense than their signs even if you sister Gee Gee no think so. When she come to visit me the car pull up and she no come in for 15 minutes. I holler thru the screen "What you doing out there?" and she say "Im reading you porch." She could be a little snot sometimes, you know. She laff but I no laff. Was lotta work makin those signs and they are all serve useful purpose. I have one with string stretch across bottom of steps say WET PAINT to keep away robbers at night, one what say NO TRESPAS BY ORDER POLIS DEPARTAMENT to keep the robbers away during the day, one for mailman what say PLEASE DELIVER MAIL TO BOX ON BACK PORCH so he believe my wet paint sign, and one what say WE ALREADY DONATE ON UNITE CRUSADE because them people walk on anything, and one by the doorbell which say BELL OUT OF ORDER in case they gonna try again anyway. For little extra strength I put one up BEWARE OF DOG. So far all works very good. The only one who is ring this bell is you little sister Gee Gee after shes finish read the porch.

I now sign off.

Love,

Uncle Ambrogio

Dear Gina,

I am recuperate now in nice quiet room in hospital. I am glad I don't remember the days in the Intense Care, only you faces bending over me which was the only good part. Thank you to Earl for bring you so fast. Everyone was good to avoid mengen what the doctor find but now it relieve you mind to know that I know and you can mengen all you want. After all, to not mengen will not make it go away. Only bout two more weeks now before I go to Stanford Hospital for the treataments. These guys are gonna make me sicker before they make me get better. You sister Gee Gee she's arrange to have house keeper for me when I go home. She is sittin with me here every day lookin at me with them cow eyes and I think by now she could use the bed across the hall. I rest now.

> Love,
>
> Your Uncle Ambrogio

Buon Giorno!

Here I am home in the house with wounderful house keeper Gee Gee has find for me name of Margaret. Almost three months in hospital sure make me glad to see this house. I sit like king and Margaret take care of everything including this darn bag what I have to wear. I can't try to walk yet even with my walker without her right next to me, but what the hell, I not going anyplace anyway. If I'm not good she's shake a finger in front of my face straighten me out. Its nice to have somebody holler to me once in while again.

Avengally the day might come when she try to make a little gnocci for me. Lets hope it dont turn out like yours which was like pieces bubble gum. I no mean to hurt you feelings, but just give you lil something to chew on for while.

I remain,

Your Uncle Ambrogio

Dear Gina,

Its about time you write to me. Maybe I'm answer too soon but I think eather now or never.

Im sorry to hear Earl still walks fonny with his broke foot but I know how to coret this limbing problem when hes walking. In order to equalize his walk you gotta hit him on the other foot. You could also stick him in a wheel chair and push him around but be careful no do what I did with Noni one time. I'm wheeling her in hospital corridor which have slight slant. I let go for minit to hold open the door for Gee Gee to follow me and the chair she get away from me and off she go. You Mother she is sitting and smile and enjoy the fast ride and not know nobody is steer. In the meantime I run like hell to catch up with her and I reach her just in time to hear her say "Is not necessary to go so fast."

I also have adventure of my own in wheel chair when I was in hospital. I can't walk but my room mate he's in pretty good shape and he take me for ride. He's Portugese man and no understand me and I no understand him, but we have hell of good time romin round that hospital. When we return the nurse she is running in panik up and down the hall because we have disappear. She bawl hell out of us and the other guy he was lucky that he couldn't understand her, but I could.

When you answer please spell like I do other wise it makes pretty rouf for me to read it most of times. I know is hard but try hard.

I remain,

Your Uncle Ambrogio

Dear Gina,

Here I am again with more story of adventure I have in the hospital. Is funny but when I was there I didn't seem to be have such good time and now I'm home and think back on things what make me laff like hell. The nurse she fix my cathater one day and I look down and see some puddle on the floor. So happens was rain very hard outside and I ask her, "Have you got leak in this roof?" Shes look up and study the cealing for few minits and she say "No, I don't think so, why?" And I say "Something sprung leek so if not the ceiling must be me."

Every time she take my pulse I laff out loud and she never know why. I don't explain to her but I explain to you. You Mother is say to me one day "My pulse she is getting very thin." This worry me because I think she mean shes feeling week and I say, "You mean you pulse is week?" and she say "No dummy — my pulse is thin" and she's put her finger round to show me. I say "You mean you wrist is get thin." and she say "Dummy, you know we got no word wrist in Italy."

When they first put me in that hospital and Gee Gee comes to see me I ask her why do they put me in room with old lady? She tole me over and over was old man with very high voice so avengally I let her think she convince me, but what the hell the difference any way — she couldn't do nothing and I couldn't do nothing. After couple days she was remove so maybe they find out I was right.

First day I am wheel out of that room I find out I'm on third floor and look out the window down on the trees I think I have plant years ago when I work on the Stanford Village. Give me the crips to see how big they are now and I am up here lookin down on them. They are grow and I am shrink.

Adio,

Uncle Ambrogio

Dear Gina,

I wish I could have dog to play round here. For some reason I have spend lot time lately think about Ebonear. You remember him the little white dog with the black ear we have many years ago when you were lil gel? He use to run thru the tall weeds on his hind leg so he could see where he was going. One time you Pop take Ebby for walk in the field and Ebby run ahead of him. In the meantime you Pop he take new eye glass out of his pock and put them on. He never have wore them before and Ebby have never see him with them on. Ebby he run back and look up and make fast stop before he start to snarl and try to bite Pop in the ankel. Pop is holler "It's me Ebby, you Daddy!" and Ebby keep bark and snarl til Pop he take off the glass from his eyes. With dog as smart as this you got to carry identificashun card at all times.

I find the box of dirt that I bring from Italy when I visit there 10 years ago. I never tell you how insult you Mother get when I bring her that. She had tell me to bring her souvenir of the old country and I think it would be nice to bring her some soil from her home ground. She holler "What I need Italian dirt for when I got plenty American dirt all over the place?" Good thing I also bring religious medal bless by Pope and one gold cross.

One good thing bout sittin here, I find plenty time to think back on all these fine memery.

Big baccione con amore.

I remain,

Your Uncle Ambrogio

Dear Gina,

Friend of mine brout me duck to roast and right away I have something to say to you bout that.

When Al had his bar lots of customers use to bring him things like the fish they catch, venison, and things like that. One time some one bring him several geese. Live one. So happen this same day Noni decide to call him at the bar just to say hello and she call him while he was with lots customer and live geese in the back room squacking. He pick up his phone say Hello and she say in cute lil voice, "Hello. Guessa who this is?" And Al say, "Eleanor Roosevelt. Godamn it, Eleanor, I told you not to bother me during the rush hour." And he hang up the phone. The steam come out of her ears to let him catch her that way. Pretty soon the phone ring and she say Hello and he say, "Hi, Ma." She say "Who is this?" in very sweet voice again. He say, "Come on, Ma, it's me, Al, your son." She say, "You must have rong number, my son name Frankaleen." And she hang up the phone. He call back and say, "Don't hang up, Ma. You want a goose?" She say, "You want slap on you lips?" He say, "I mean a real goose." and she say, "I mean a real slap on you lips." And she hang up the phone again. I say, "Why you keep hang up on him?" She say, "I have no time for stranger. I'm busy run the country."

He brought her the goose and I bring you the story.

Adio,

Uncle Ambrogio

Dear Gina,

I find one lettera today that you write to me several years ago and it make me laff so much. You explain bout the time Wendy she was 3 year old and she was playin out in the snow and every few minit she ring the front door bell and be pest. You figure the next time the bell ring you gonna get on you knees and then open the door and holler to her "What you want?" So the bell ring again and you get on you knees and walk on them to the door and pull it open and holler to insurance man's knees, "What you want?"

Same lettera tell bout the man who come to the door and say "I make all the women on this block — what day you want me to make you?" and you are relieve to see he is drive delicatessin truck.

My garden is get to be mess now. I see the lily what I transplant all surround by weed. When Noni ask me to transplant that thing couple year ago was very big and should be divide, and I ask her "Do you want me to transplant the whole thing?" and that smart mouth she say "No, joost the top half, that is the only part what show anyway."

Everything I look at here bring back a story. When she buy these books on the shelve the salesman come to the door with them. She no want him to know she can't read so she stare at them pages long time sayin 'Hmmmm — Uh huh — Oh yes" and so on. She had him very nervouse before she bought a few. I use to read them to her when she can't watch TV much any more because her eye bother her, and also they fill my time now.

Father Moran comes today so I make sure I swear a lot before he get here. What the Hell, I got to have something to confess, dont I? Other wise he is waste a trip.

I remain,

Your Uncle Ambrogio

Dear Gina,

I am glad that you are feeling fine and now I want to have the pleasure to tell you that I am feeling fine too.

I am writing right away to tell you bout the recipe I send you few weeks ago for curing olives. I forget to mengen that if it still taste bitter after you take them out of the lye and leave in water only one day it could kill you. If that is the case, soak them in clear water at least one more day, maybe two.

Today Margaret went to the store and Gee Gee was here keep me company. She put me in the big chair and park my walker across the room. Then she go outside for something and lock herself out, and I can't let her in because I don't have my walker and I can't reach it. We look at each other thru the window like couple dummies til Margaret get back from the store. It remind me of the time I am putting tar on the roof and Al doesn't know I am up there and he take away the ladder and leave for the afternoon and I am strand up there til he comes back several hours later.

Please don't believe anything I have said.

Con Amore.

I remain,

Your Uncle Ambrogio

Dear Gina,

Here is lil something to cheer up you day, which will cheer up mine. I find this picture of you Mother which she have taken when Albert was in the army. She put bandage all over herself, head rap up and arm in sling with splint on leg, and she ask me to send it to him with the message: "Dear Son, everything is fine at home. Love, Ma."

If you happen to have a day now and then when you think you may be lil bit pazzo, you will know where you inharit it from.

Love,

Uncle Ambrogio

Dear Gina,

Wish I could sit outside on the porch at night like we use to. One time you Mother and me we were sitting out there admire the sky and she make a wish on airplane. She thout it was a moving star.

In Illinois we use to sit under the pergola and I play my accordion. There were grape vine over us and when I finish a song and ask how everyone like it a worm happen to fall on Rose's neck and she let out scream and jump up and Noni say, "It wasn't that good."

I learn National Antem and Noni say I should play it standing up. I had nuff trubel to play it sitting down.

I spend the afternoon listen to Pat Cooper and he have the capacity to cover all the Italians on one record. I enjoy that guy even if he is lil pazzo.

Say, do you think you can find the old Nofrio record? I'm afraid is too late but give a try anyway.

I quit now so you can go try.

Gu bai,

Your Uncle Ambrogio

I can not find my copy of the tape of Noni singing Silent Night. You know the one that goes "Silenna Night, Holy Night, all is common, all is brite."

Dear Gina,

They are having terible weather in Illinois, making me glad we come to California all these years. Do you remember that trip? You should since you were almost 18 already at the time, but Gee Gee she was just lil one and you take care of her all the way. Al was drive and sing the whole way, and Noni was eat oranges fast as she can when she find out we can't bring fruit in to this state and we had whole case of them with us. When we get to the border in Trukee the polisman say to Al "You got any fruit or nuts in this car?" and Al say "No fruit, but there are couple of nuts in the back seat."

It was thrill for Noni to see moundain again since she have not seen them since Italy, and she go Ooh and Aah all the way. We have Ebonear in the car with us, and that dog was blame all the way for lot of things he dont do. We never figure out who had the stomach ache.

When we got here it was the first time we move in to a house which we don't build ourself.

Gee Gee is mad at me because yesterday I forgot to take my pills all day and today I make up for it by take two of everything.

I miss you,

Uncle Ambrogio

Dear Gina,

I'm thinkin a lot about Noni all day today. Can't get her off my mind and I want you to know some of the wounderful thing she did when you kids were small and maybe dont remember.

She had on her dining tabel a big beautiful punch bowl she bring from the old country. For many years we have to be very careful of that bowl. No one was allow to wash it but her and no one go near it without worry bout it. When you kids do you homework at that tabel you were so careful not to be too close to that bowl. One night you and Rose were sit there doing rithmatic for school and you by accident happen to bump that bowl. You dont hurt it but you get so scare you start to cry and Noni she look so shock at you. She give you kees and then she pick up that bowl, carry it to the back porch and drop it over the rail to the cement below where it smash in million piece. She come back kees you once more and say "Now you enjoy this tabel." I ask her why didn't she just put it away some place and she say "Because they think there is still something in the house more important than they are. This way they know for sure it doesn't count." Then she went clean up all the glass.

When we first finish build that house and move in we were first Italian family there and the neighbor they don't approach us for long time. Avengally whenever some one they get sick or need help they run to you Mother and she go with soup and help them what ever way she can. During World War 2 I dont think any boy left that town without come for spaghetti dinner first, and she cry over many of them who did not come back. Keep these memery like treasure because they become more valuble as you get older.

I remain,

Your Uncle Ambrogio

Dear Gina,

I spend a pleasent Sunday at Gee Gee apartamente which is very big for apartamente. More like flat. And now I'm laffing because I am remind of when I tell Noni that the Walker family they live in a flat and she say, "A flat what?" I say, "A flat is like house with nother house on top of it" and she say "No wonder is flat."

While there visiting with Cow Eyes I watch on TV Roy Roger and Dale Evan talking and I think how Noni use to love to watch them, and she like the song they sing at the end. Whenever some one they leave the house, stead of say Good Luck she say "Happy Trella to you" and they don't know what she mean but they say "Thank you, and the same to you."

She also use to say to people "You Bastia,"* and they think she say "You betcha." I pull few sneeker like that myself, special when I would drive away from gas station in car that was still running lousy, and the mechanik he say "Thank you." I say "You bastia." It pays to be Italian. Noni say that to. The only thing worse than be Italian is to not be Italian. Remember that. I don't know what it will get you, but remember that any way.

Remember also to answer this.

Your Uncle Ambrogio

*Beast

Dear Gina,

Couple of guys who used to work with me come to visit today. One they call Dummy and one is name Ercole. Dummy got his name because he use to walk round the grounds pushing his wheel barrell upside down. I didn't think that was so dum because that way no one can put anything in it. They check around the house to see if they can fix anything for me and they are nice guys to do that, don't you think?

I also get phone call from Uncle Sam long distance which was nice of him to do that. Nobody was on the extension here this time. Remember when you call Noni and me from Los Angeles and we are each on different phone on this end and she and I start to talk to each other and you are sittin in Los Angeles listen to us?

I sure had good time when I was there to visit you. I never forget that Disneyland, which is something to see. That Abrahem Lincone statue is just a dummy and he talk better than I do. I wish Noni could have see that place. It has been several year and I still can pitcher that whole place in my mind.

I hear some noise in the house last night but cant be robber because what do they want here? One time when you Momma and I come home from Gee Gee's we come in the door and think we hear noise in the back of house so she say in loud voice "Don't worry if it is a robber because you got you gun." And like big dumbell I holler "What good is gun without bullit?" I got a hit on the head for that one. Love and kees.

I remain,

Your Uncle Ambrogio

Dear Gina,

They are load some stuff from a truck outside and I'm thinking on the time you Pop was direct one truck driver who was backing up to plate glass front. Pop sees he is get close to the window and he wave his arms and yell very excite "La fenestra! La fenestra!"* and the driver think hes yell "Faster!" "Faster!" and he crash throu.

Al did this on purpose once to friend of his who was try to drive on to grease pit in garage. Al is say "lil more — lil more" and the car she fall frontward right in the pit. Those guys they do some terrible things to each other and they laff at the rong time. They have baseball game and Al and Andy are sittin in the stand watchin, and just as guy hit the ball Andy holler "Down in front" and the guy in front of him get down and Andy get hit in the mouth with the ball, knok out all his front teeth, and Al is laffing all the way to the doctor with him. God get even with Al when he was running down the hall at school with books under his arms and hands in his pocks and he fall and slide on his face and can't get the hands out of his pocks. He chip two teeth in front and Andy laff like hell bout that.

Do you remember the time Al, Andy and Art they come home with live ducks and throw them on the bed where you and Rose are sleepin? You were scream and the ducks were quack and Noni get up and start yellin. Those guys were devil, but at least they don't have no drug or booze, and the polis laff with them. If that happen now they would go to penitenchary for life. Then they would be write the letters.

Adio con amore.

I remain,

Your Uncle Ambrogio

*The window! The window!

Dear Gina,

Guess what I see on the TV tonight? The same spook story that you and Gee Gee see the night you scare hell out of each other. It have the spooky song in it, and after you went to bed and each thout the other was asleep, you try to remember the song so you hum it soft to youself and she let out scream which scare you and you let out scream and everybody in the house jump and run. The only one who didn't run out was the dog Leroy who was hide under the bed cryin.

Now I think of the time you scare Noni so bad. You were come home later than you should from date and you sneek in throu the basement and up the stairs and you hear Noni in the kitchen so you sit on the step to wait til she go to bed and you fall asleep. She open the door and see body there and she let out scream and everybody find out how late you get home.

Now that make me think of the time you and Rose don't get home from party til 6:00 in the morning and you Pop he catch you in the kitchen all dress up. Rose is quick thinkin and she say "We decide to get up and go look for job this morning." Pop he say "That's good girls" and after he leave for work you both go to bed.

One thout lead to nother, dont they?

I remain,

Your Uncle Ambrogio

Dear Gina,

Polis were in front to chase away some kids what was foolin round cross the street and I sit in the window and watch the show. This show came to me stead of me go to it like I do one time. Noni and me we were drivin to Gee Gee's apartment and I see line of cars to right of road and several polismens there and I want to know what is going on so I say to Noni "I turn back and find out what is goin on." She say "Mind you own business" and I say "I want to see what is goin on", so I turn round and go back and pretty soon I find out what is goin on. I find out I need new tail light and front light adjustment because I am in trafic check. I also find out Noni enjoy this very much. If they have place like this for human bodies I would go get in line again.

Remember when Noni she had to be in traction each day for several hour, and I put the strap under her chin and raise her head up by pully attach to door frame? I am putting her there one day when Gee Gee call and say "What are you doin?" and I say "I'm hang you Mother in the dining room." Gee Gee laff like crazy because shes know what I mean but you Mother can't laff because her jaws were tie together. She got one treat to eat after her treatment and I ask her "You want cookie, piece pound cake or dish of ice cream?" and she say "Yes." She never let me put her in that traction before noon because every morning about 11:00 that tall skinny neighbor Ida walk by with her nose in the air and Noni have to watch her because she say one of these day Ida is gonna trip and fall and she no wanna miss it.

I did one more painting of birds this week. I show one bird just looking, one just listening and one pulling on a worm which I label it "Success."

Adio, big baccione con amore.

I remain,

Your Uncle Ambrogio

Dear Gina,

Al was visit me this morning and he is still full of the bolony and funny story like always was. He recall one time when he sneak out the upstairs window to stay out all night. Was winter time and he leave the window open slight bit so he could push his way in when he come home. In the meantime while he was gone the window they froze like that, so he get home and climb up the tree to the roof where he is very careful to inch his way up the slant which was very slippery. When he get to the top he put his hands against the window and give a push and push himself right off the roof. Was a good thing he land in the snow and even at that he hurt hisself pretty good. What a devil.

I receive the pumpkin bread you send me and I thank you with the bottom of my heart.

Uncle Ambrogio

Dear Gina,

Gee Gee is here today cleanin round in the basament and once in while I hear squealin and happy noise from down there. She find Noni's old canning jars with rubber rings and iron lid and tell me they are anteek, and do you want her to save some them for you? I think I have bunch junk down there and she makes treazure out of it. Then she bawl me out for getting rid of the old pedal sewing machine because was anteek also. The best this does is give me assurance that she will never get rid of me because in few more years I will be priceless treazure.

Also consorning the old papers and things in the trunk I want to know do you want them? I have beautiful drawings and paintings done by Rose some which I have frame and some I save for each of you. Rose say take what you want because she still does the drawing and painting and makes more for herself.

I gonna black mail Gee Gee with one picture I find of her with me which was take few years back. I am stand behind her and she is look so glamrous while I am pretend to look for kootie in her hair. Seein her like lil pak rat round here remind me of when Noni use to bake all those cookie and Gee Gee she take few of them home in a sack. Was gunny sack.

She is here starin at me now with them big cow eyes of hers and I can not concetrate on this no more so I sign out with one big baccione, lot of love, and basament full of jars.

Uncle Ambrogio

Dear Gina,

I thank you for the Easter bread you send even though it is not Easter. Everyone came over to sneck on some and we made an Easter out of it. Which remind me of our big Easter dinner we always have with everyone round. Al always eat so much that he can hardly leave the tabel and he barely make it to the living room and lay down on the floor on his back to recover. Remember the time he fell asleep on the bed and you put a lily in his hands? That was the time he brought that crazy friend of his to have dinner with us — guy name of Marty who talk like a fool at the tabel. He say they should take all the black people and all the Jews and put them on a boat and take them to Island, and Noni she say "And I know who should be drivin the boat." He shut up after that. We never see him again which was fine.

Gee Gee call me every day if she is not here with me and today when she call I tell her to wait til Margaret bring me my glasses so I can hear better and I don't know why she laff because it is true. I had one friend of mine who cant dance without his glass on his eyes and he does not watch his feet either. You better put yours on to figure out this lettera.

Arrividerci, resposto pronto.

I remain,

Your Uncle Ambrogio

Dear Gina,

I'm going to write to you today stead of read the paper. You really gotta be in the mood to read the paper these days. You got to feel like be miserabel. I remember the time when in order to read it I had to stand on the kitchen floor and look down. These days the paper they belong spread out on the floor, because that is all they are good for. Everybody is kill everybody and I think the reason for this is there is not enuf strickness with the parent. In my time when one of us do something rong, who ever was the one near to my Father get a good wack on the head. This was enuf to straighten out all of us, but of course we took turns sit next to him. We took care of sickness by wear string of garlic round our neck which make sense to me and will to you too if you think about it for minit. We also pray a lot all the time. Mama she use to have her own lil alter in the bedroom and she go there to pray when ever she have chance. If she is busy she say to God "You gotta scuse me for now til lunch" and He would.

Today everything she is done by some book. Even the cookin no come natural to the women. They gotta read every move they make. You Mama was cook with five sifters flour, flat hands salt, round hands suger and give a smell and a pinch, and everything was good. When we have restarant she cook for all those people each day and never be nervous. Trubel with her was she go round to all the tabels and ask if they had enuf to eat and sometimes fill up plates 2 or 3 time, which is why we go out of business. I'm going to read the paper now. Lots of kees.

I remain,

Your Uncle Ambrogio

Dear Gina,

Here I am slow but shure with some nothing to say. I have receive the pictures of beautiful Wendy and beautiful Lori. They sure looking good and I keep them on dining room table so I can look every time I gone by.

I have send you the califlower bread recipe and now I find the second half of the recipe she is still here with me. I hope you no try to make it. I now enclose the second part. Stupido me.

Father Moran keep on coming every Friday of the month like he did when Noni was here until the lest time when I told him he no have to come that often. He say "You want to be saved don't you?" and I say "Yes, Father, put me in the frizer."

Today Yola and Gee Gee are here for all day and Yola is fix wounderful dinner which we are all eat it together. Janice and Michael are here too and I sure enjoy them kids. Yola and Jim got lots to be proud. Janice and Gee Gee is busy all night put my paintings in frames for putting round the house. They sure are lookin good.

I know you can read all this scrabbling because you are almost as smart as I am.

I remain,

Your Uncle Ambrogio

Dear Gina,

On way to the doctor today we pass by what use to be the 4-0 restaurant which we have run during the war. Noni she did all that fine cookin in there, Al was tend bar and you girls all help round. I wish I could go look in that kitchen to see if the cleaver mark is still in the wall from the time Noni throw it at the guy who went noseying in her kitchen.

Do you remember when the robber came in and was point the gun at Al and the other bartender say "You don't have the nerve to shoot" and Al say "You got the nerve, you got the nerve, I believe you Buddy." Then the robber run with the money and Al jump in his car and chase him while we call polis, and the polis they catch Al and let the robber get away. Them was the good old day, boy. We were rob several time, but that one was the most fun to remember.

You girls were pinch so many time by customers you finally put sign on you shoulders "The bartender is my brother. Think before you pinch." They can see right away Al is pretty big guy, and lot of thinkin and no pinchin went on after that.

Al did beautiful singin while serve drinks and most request he have was for "When Irish Eyes Smiling" and he feel like such traiter to the wops he use to cross himself each time before he sing it. Did you know he win amature contest when he is 15 years old, singin the song "Trees"? You know how she goes, "I think that I shall never see pome lovly like a tree." And Yola also win beauty contest when she is 15, but Pop no let her take the prize which was trip to Holly Wood for movies test. We had our own Frank Sinatra and Hedi Lemar.

Kees to you,

Uncle Boo

Dear Gina,

I would like to clear out some of the furniture here in the house to make it easier for me to get around in my wheelchair. First I want to ask is there anything you want to keep or give it to somebody. We have the two couch in the living room and only one is necessary, so I think I get rid of the big one. Was beautiful when was new even tho it did not cost very much but it should have. When Noni buy it she give the man such a bad time he was glad to get rid of it. She keep after him argue, argue til he finally give up and say "O.K. you can have it cheaper" and she say, "Why? What's rong with it?" He say "Nothing is rong with it." She say, "Then why you sell it cheap?" I don't remember how much he took off, but what he lose in money he gain in experience.

I was do the gardening work in my spare time then and people they would call the house with jobs for me to do. One woman who call was one who brag all the time that everything in her house was imported. Noni don't like her too much, and she take the call. When she realize who she is talking to she up my price quite a bit and the woman ask why is Bruno's price so much higher than anyone else? Noni say, "Because he is imported." She hire me anyway.

This same woman she get very walthy from real estate she work in, and once when we were discusing her, Al he say, 'She got good head on her shoulder" and Noni say "Must be — it has two faces on it."

Comes time to shut up so you can let me know bout furniture.

Lots kees,

Your Uncle Ambrogio

Dear Gina,

Al say don't tell you this, which is a good sign, so I sit right down and tell you pronto. When he was first married, his wife she come to Noni all upset crying, "Mama, Mama, Al he want to go out every night when he get off work and we fight bout it and I don't know what to do." Noni say, "Bigga deal — whats so tuff bout that? He have to have clothes to go out, don't he? So you justa take all his pants out of the cloz and you tear them in half." Which she did right away, and Al come with mouth open to Noni, hold his pants on his arm and say, "Look what she did to my pants." And Noni she say, "If you was get too big for them, what you want keep them for anyway?" Al he leave like sheep and his wife say "Thank you, Mama" and their divorce was put off ten years. Even after the ten years his wife she still call Noni often to say "I miss you, Mama. I love you Mama" and I am sure she mean it.

If you plan to tell Al I tell you this you let me know in advance so I can get head start in my wheelchair.

> I miss you Gina.
> I love you Gina.
>
> Uncle Ambrogio

Dear Gina,

Here I'm bright early in the morning to tell you some good news. Gary and Barbaruccia were here last night and be back tomorrow. I sure enjoy them. Gary have pick out very nice wife and she is also Barbarella — which mean pretty Barbara. They took me to the medico yesterday and he pronounce me fearly good heath Dago and I did not believe him for sentimendal reason. I do feel better, but not hell of a lot.

The box of kum quat have arrived yesterday in good order. I have nippled on them and they are very tasty. I send kees to everyone incluting Earl.

Tocca a lei ora,*

Uncle Ambrogio

*It is your turn now.

Dear Gina,

Scuse all past complaint I make that I don't have picture of all five you kids together because I just find one. Was taken at Gee Gee wedding of all four you girls with Albert. I am so happy to find this, and after several day of studying it carefuly I have come to conclushun which I place before you now — This is a fine looking bunch of wops.

Love,

Uncle Ambrogio

Dear Gina,

Do you have the lady come sell perfume and lipstick by you house? If not, we have one here you can have. She come ding dong once in while even tho she know there is no one here but me. I have helluva time to get to the door and when I find her stand there I would love to get mad on her, but she smile so nice I have not manage to yet.

I sure do miss Mr. Moscowitz. Years ago he would come around with his truck which had everything in it for whole house including clothes. He would holler at the back porch "Mr. Moscowitz!" and Noni holler back "Hello Moscowitz!" and she go out and look over the things to see what she need. One time she bought something she didn't know what it was. She hang it in the kitchen and when each one come in that night and say "What is that thing?" she say "That's none you business." I say to her, "If you don't know what it is, why you buy it?" She say, "That's none you business." It hang there for 20 years and we never find out what it was. It had wire on it and handle made of metal. Don't ask me any more bout it because that's none you business.

In the meantime, kiss everybody for me, and I mean business.

Con Amore,

Uncle Ambrogio

Dear Gina,

I just get home from doctor where I go to have the garden hose removed. When the examination was over I told him to take 4 tabelspoon Milk Magnesia 8 times day for 3 months then call me and let me know how he feel. I for the first time walk with cane and I did pretty good. Of course the nurse hold me on one hand while we are walking. I say to her "I wish I never get well." She say "Why?" and I tell her "Because I like to hold you hand for long time." Then I think I better back off a little bit because I remember shes sinkle. But don't get me wrong blobbity mouth, because I am feeling fine.

When I arrive home I am greeted by mouse in the kitchen and I am so glad to see him there. He's cute lil one and will liven up the place which could use it. He makes me think of that hampster what Wendy and Lori have when they are tiny and how they loved that lil thing.

I been getting letter from Lori every day and I love to. Shes sure nice ragazza.* So is also your Wendy. Che e bella! Give them kees from their Uncle Ambrogio.

Thats me.

*girl

Dear Gina,

Today I find in bottom of the buffet drawer two framed pictures which Noni used to have out all the time. They are one of the Pope and one of Gorjes George. I laff like hell when I see them because they are in matching frame and use to be next to each other when she was watch the old wrastling match on the TV. She was get so excite over them match and yell and bang the table next to her, and if she cuss at George she pologize to the Pope at the same time. I could never convince her that was all put up job and he was fony. I mean George, not the Pope. The table still have the scratch and mark where she bang the ash tray down when she cuss them out. This way she could look from one picture to another while she yell, "You sonama bitch" and "Scuse me". Sometime she go so fast she get mix up and call the Pope a sonama bitch. I think I put them frames back out and put in the new Pope and the President, and I pick up where she leave off.

The boy I hire to clean the yard come this morning and he is just young kid with first job. He was worry that he don't do good enough work and I give him the same advice I got years ago. Just try to fill the back of the shovel and the front will take care of itself. The same to you.

Adio,

Uncle Ambrogio

Dear Gina,

I am sorry I never learn about the game football, because I shure would have plendy to do now watchin it on TV. A bunch of young healthy guys are spending the afternoon falling on top of each other and I don't know why. The ball she is always on the bottom and maybe that is why it isn't round any more.

I wish you were here to play morra with me, or maybe briscola or three-seven. Also 7-1/2. . . you remember that one? If my memery is corret, you owe me one billion dollar from losing on you last visit. Dont bother to send it because I don't have time to count it.

Winter she is closing in and I will soon have the wounderful opportunity to see all the flowers die in the front and the leaves fall off the tree. The squirrel they have lost the battel because the walnut tree is bare this year. I am anxious to see the stupid look on their face when they arrive. Maybe I put a sign out "Out of business" for them. On the other hand maybe I have Margaret buy a few nuts and put them out in case they got family to feed and are depend on me like they always have. Them poor things, they got no unemployment line to go stand in.

School she start soon and the kids will be pestin round and it will' be good to hear the brakes squealin again. Some time the quiet is very loud round here and the noise soften it a little.

I enjoy very much to hear from you and send love to everyone.

Uncle Ambrogio

Dear Gina,

   Gee Gee of the Cow Eyes stop by to see me today and she have little kitten in her pocket and she is all upset because she can't keep it in her apartamente. So you see she is still bringing things home with her. She use to come every day with something. Once a dog, once a cat. Noni would watch her coming cross the street from school every day and she say, "She got something? Mama Mia, she got something." Noni give home to them all, whatever it was. Then one day comes Gee Gee holding the hands of girl her own age. She bring her in the house and say "Mom, this is Cindy. She have to quit school just before graduation because her Mother die and her Father can't manage." Noni say, "No, she don't. Go get the clothes." And Cindy she stay with us til she graduate with Gee Gee. She was nice girl, that Cindy. Do you remember her or was you already gone at the time? She is marry now with nice family of her own.
   I lieve you with my pen, but never with my heart,

                    Give beeg kees to you nice family for
                    Uncle Ambrogio

Dear Gina,

Today I have successful day. I have sell my car just by put sign on it in the driveway. A man come to my door and ask me the price and I say $400. He say can I come down little bit and I say O.K. — $350 and he say he takes it and he take it just like that. I'm thinking why didn't I say $375, but is too late now. He did not even look at the motor or nothing. Far as he know I could have sell the engine separate.

This remind me of when I go buy it myself. I don't know that on this car the engine is in the back and I walk around the front of this car and scratch my head while looking to open the hood which is not there. The salesman he is watching me, so not to feel like dam fool I say I was just get the feel of the ground round it. This seem to satisfy him which shows he is just as much stupido as me.

On days like this when I feel like stupido I think on the story of Mike and Ike which I hear in World War I when I am in the American Army. Mike and Ike they are workin on the railroad. Ike is kneel down and hold the spike and Mike is stand behind him with the sledge hammer in the air. Ike say, "O.K. when I am nod my head, you hit it." That is the end of Ike.

This is the end of this lettera.

Always I remain,

Your Uncle Ambrogio

Dear Gina,

It has been rain for couple days here and what come to my mind is the rain barrel we always have sitting out when we were in the old house in Illinois. You girls use that water to wash the hair because was soft water, then rinse with vinegar and water. You smell like salad, but the hair was shiny and beautiful. I remember one time Yola and Al have big fight. They was very small then and have such temper with each other. She got so mad at him and was chase him round the house and can't catch him. She finally throw a glass bottle at him but miss and it break on the ground ahead of him. He turn to holler to her "Ha ha, you miss me" and he step on the broke glass and cut his foot very bad. Yola she panic and grab him and sit him on the edge of that barrel and stick his foot in it. Noni hear all the yelling and screaming and she came out to find him sitting with his dirty foot in the rain water and Yola crying. After she fix Al's foot she give them both a good one for spoil her rain water.

I have visit from that nice German lady who use to live next block. The first time she came to visit Noni and me she bring delicious coffee cake and was very good to us. When she leave I say to Noni, "Aint she sweet?" and Noni say, "No, she's German." I told her bout that today and she had a good laff a little late. But it is never too late for laff, is it?

Big baccione,

Uncle Ambrogio

Dear Gina,

I watch Frank Sinatra last night on the TV and think its shame that he don't know how Noni use to stick up for him. She watch him very proud because he was nice Italian boy and when anyone say something bad about him she say, "You no pick on Frank Sinatra in my house." and they shut up. How he got along without her all these years I don't know. She was worry about how skinny he was too.

When we have the restaurant do you remember how she use to worry bout the customer all the time? She came out from the kitchen and went round to all the tables asking them if they had enuf to eat, offer them recipes. Specially the skinny people.

When she made the ciamella and was not suppose to eat them she made sure to have some with very big holes that she could slip on her wrist, and she wear them and snip off little at a time and chew on it when nobody was looking. But I was looking anyway. One time she had hide in her pock several candy. Was like living in house with pick pock. I say "What you got in you pock?" She say "What pock?" I say "You only got one pock" and she say "Mine you own business." I say "You want to get sick?" She say "You want get lots trouble?" I drop the subject and she continue to sneak the candy to them lips. Then Gee Gee come in later and say, "Mom, you allow to have one candy tonight." and she act so innocent and say, "Oh, I preciate very much to have one candy. Thank you." And then she look at me to keep my mouth shut. With all the experience I have behind me I could become expert crook. I can look innocent in any situation.

> For now I close this situation.
> Con Amore,
>
> Your Uncle Ambrogio

Dear Gina,

It's too bad you are not here to smell my spaghetti sauce. Use you imaginashun and figure it smell a lil better than yours does and you will come close. Just sitting here smelling it brout to my mind a few spaghetti stories.

During World War 2 Noni use to make spaghetti dinners for all the boys who were leave for the Army. She start that to keep you busy and take you mind off that boy you use to write to every night and cry you eyes out. Then she begin to enjoy it very much herself, even if it dint help you out any. She would set the big table load with food and we all sit there for hours and enjoy. One time when Gee Gee Cow Eyes was baby she fall asleep at the table and her head drop down with her face in the spaghetti. To not interupt the dinner Noni just turn her face gently so only her head was in it, and we finish dinner.

One time Noni she call Navy Pier in Chicago and tell them if they have any lonesum boys who like to have family meal to send them over. Next Sunday come 8 sailors and they had a heck of good time for themself, playing ball in the field next door and eat at the picnic table under the tree. Do you remember that day? I think for sure the boys they remember that. One neighbor critisize her for the noise those boys make that day and for having so many strange sailor there and Noni agree with her. She say, "You right 100 percent. If those boys they are willing to go get kill for people like you, then they are strange, all right." Then she tell her to go home and she went.

Now I go and eat.

Uncle Ambrogio

Dear Gina,

I fill my time now paint the pictures and do the puzzle and play checker with Margaret. Is hard for me to lift my accordian up so I don't play any more but a lot times I play the small organ when I want to make music.

I am sorry my lettera not so long but I go lay down to rest several times during the day and I don't finish between one rest and another. I enjoy to look out the window. Have I tell you the boy is back walking by the window every day at the same time and we wave to each other. I look forward to see him each day but I don't know his name, and he does not know mine.

The flower in front are bloom and so are the weeds. I would enjoy to go out there and pull them.

My nap is due again so I close with lot love to all of you.

I remain,

Your Uncle Ambrogio

Dear Gina,

Would you like to have Noni's watch? It does not work but is nice to look at and you can wear it on the days when you don't care what time it is. Al give it to her but he no longer has a wife to claim it. When he give it to her he say, "Stick with me, Bubbles, and you will be wear dimonds." and Noni say, "They make stret jacket with dimond now?" But she love the watch and continue to wear it when it stop working.

Also the stachoo of Jesus which she use to talk to is still here. She kept it in her bedroom and when ever something bad happen to her she go in and say, "I give you chance to explain and if its not good explainashun I talk to you Father." When Gary was in Vietnam she talk to God lots. She did not believe you when you say Gary was in Hawaii. She knew where he was all the time. When he would write her lettera tell her big story bout the palm tree and how nice it was there she say, "Dont tell him I know where he is because he have nuff to worry already." When he came home safe she make sure to go in the bedroom to say thank you, and she cry lil bit while smiling. She tole me once that the stachoo smile on her. I say, "You crazy, I never saw that stachoo smile." She say, "I dint say He smile on you—I say He smile on me."

Con Amore,

Your Uncle Ambrogio

My Dear Sweethearta,

     I want you to have this poem.

From three tiny seeds I fashioned it
My garden of memory
Blossom to blossom
Full shrub to tree
From snowflake to raindrop
I bent to their need
Knowing the dreams in my heart would look back
There for my eyes to see
Faith hope and charity
Guarding the growing thing
Beauty forever for me
I'm glad that I planted those tiny seeds
In my garden of memory

     You like it Gina?
     I wish I wrote it.

                    Love,
                    Uncle Ambrogio

Dear Gina,

I am feeling very good to get your lettera telling me you want to put my lettera in book. It give me chance to leave mark of some kind when I am gone, even if it is small one someplace. You Mother have say to me many times before she have gone that she is not leaving mark of any kind on the world, and I am telling her she will leave five children and that is plenty good enouf mark, and maybe they make a few mark of their own which they could not do if she did not put them there in the first place. The most of us, instead of good mark, we leave mess behind, so every little mark she will help out a little bit. Then maybe when God take a look at our report card and He see lot of good mark there He decide to keep the school open a little longer.

You see I am not such good filosfer like I am not good speller but the meaning is what count, and the simple word what are the best. So I leave you now with simple word goodbye with big baccione which you pass on to everyone there, and that is even better than words.

I remain,

Your Uncle Ambrogio